DREAM AGAIN

DREAM AGAIN

TOMMY BARNETT

WITH LELA GILBERT

CREATION
HOUSE
Orlando, FL

DREAM AGAIN by Tommy Barnett with Lela Gilbert
Published by Creation House
Strang Communications Company
600 Rinehart Road
Lake Mary, Florida 32746
Web site: http://www.creationhouse.com

Unless otherwise noted, all Scripture quotations are from the King James Version of the Bible.

Scripture quotations marked RSV are from the Revised Standard Version of the Bible. Copyright © 1946, 1952, 1971 by the Division of Christian Education of the National Council of the Churches of Christ in the USA. Used by permission.

Scripture quotations marked NIV are from the Holy Bible, New International Version. Copyright © 1973, 1978, 1984, International Bible Society. Used by permission.

Some of the names in the stories have been changed to protect the privacy of the individuals.

Library of Congress Cataloging-in-Publication Data
Barnett, Tommy.
    Dream again / by Tommy Barnett.
        p. cm.
    ISBN: 0-88419-523-6 (pbk.)
    1. Christian life—Assemblies of God authors. I. Title
BV4515.2.B287   1998   98-20156
289.9'4—dc21   CIP

89012345 BBG 8765432
Printed in the United States of America

Dedicated to all the wonderful deacons and leaders of Phoenix First Assembly who have stood with me. They are risktakers who believed in the dream and allowed me to dream. Dedicated also to all people who believe in the dream and have given sacrificially, allowing the dream to come into fruition.

Without a dream, people perish
Without the people, the dream perishes . . .

Introduction

THE WORLD HAS BEEN SHAPED AND TRANSFORMED BY THE dreams and visions of every generation. Christopher Columbus had a dream—he envisioned a new country that would be dedicated to God. Henry Ford had a dream—a car that every person could afford. Martin Luther King had a dream—a nation in which all races and creeds could come together. The list of visionaries who have changed the world is endless. We would be uncivilized, uneducated, and perhaps even unconverted to Christ without the dreamers who have gone before us.

I've spent a lot of time studying dreamers. My library is filled with books about dreamers—especially preachers of days gone by—and I've learned that they were all different. Some were bombastic. Some preached softly (the most spiritual of all had raspy voices and thinning hair—like me!). Every great man of God has been unique, but they have had one thing in common: They've all had a dream. Preachers, then and now, have a dream to lift you out of yourself into another Self that is greater than yourself—to lead you to Christ, from whom abundant life flows even in the face of the most difficult circumstances.

You never know what you can accomplish unless you have a dream. "Without a dream," the Bible says, "people perish." (See Proverbs 29:18.) Nations perish. Cities perish. Churches perish. Without a dream, hope dies. Why do kids turn to drugs, knowing those drugs will kill them? Why do they turn to gangs when they know the gang lifestyle will destroy them and their families? Why do people turn to the bottle? To crime? Even to suicide? They turn away from life and health because they have lost all hope.

People have no hope because they've lost their dreams. Burnout does not come from overwork; burnout comes from dream deprivation. Some of the people you'll read about in this book are dreaming their first dream; others have watched their dream die and are learning to dream again. These stories are full of hope—because you can never despair as long as you can dream.

As God's people, we have to be wise about our dreams. We don't want to pursue false hopes or fantasies that feed our selfishness, our lust, or our greed. As followers of Jesus Christ, we want Him to place *His* dreams in our hearts.

How can you know if your dream is from God? I believe there are at least three questions you can ask yourself to be sure.

First, *is the dream bigger than you are?* If the dream is bigger than your ability to accomplish it, then it's God's dream, and God will get the glory. We need to let God's people dream big. Sometimes when we hear about a Christian brother's or sister's vision for achieving something grand, we secretly think, *I hope God will humble them.* That's backward. God's people ought to be the biggest dreamers in the world. Jesus told twelve ordinary people to reach the world with the gospel, *and they did.* Why should we expect to do anything less?

Second, *can you let it go?* Dreams are illusive. They get away. You become disillusioned, and soon the doubt peddlers come. People don't support you; they try to put you in a box. Finally you let go of the dream—but if it's God's dream, it won't let go of you! You may even try to escape it, but its grip is too sure.

I dreamed of starting a ministry in Los Angeles for forty years. Despite innumerable setbacks, frustrations, and disappointments, I could never get away from that dream. I know from experience: If it's God's dream, you won't be able to let it go, and eventually it will come to pass. Read on to find out what's happening at our Dream Center in L.A.

Third, *are you willing to die for it?* Are you willing to give your life, or even more difficult—to give your children's lives for the dream? I wrestled with this question when I had to decide whether my son Matthew should go to inner-city Los Angeles to head up the Dream Center. I remembered that God so loved the world that He gave His Son (John 3:16). Did I love Los Angeles enough to give my son? I'd give my life, but would I give my Matthew? Today my wife and I have given our son to Los Angeles so that God will have many more sons for Himself.

Do you have a dream? In this collection of true stories, you will read about dozens of people—people not unlike yourself—who have experienced God's touch upon their dreams. One thing we know is that His ways are usually not our ways. But He has promised, if we are willing to trust Him, to give us the desires of our hearts (Ps. 37:4). That's what He has done in the lives of the dreamers whose stories you are about to read. That's what He's done for me. And that's what He'll do for you.

Electric Train Dream

CHRISTMAS IS A TIME OF DREAMS COME TRUE FOR SOME children and a time of broken dreams for others. In the hope that we can reach some of the neediest children in our community, both our Phoenix church, Phoenix First Assembly of God, and our Los Angeles Dream Center provide more than ten thousand Christmas gifts for local children every year. The people who donate the presents are instructed not to spend less than five dollars, but to invest as much more than five dollars as they feel they can. They are to mark their package for a boy or a girl and place it at the side of our church tree. The children, who are brought to church by our fleet of buses, randomly receive their gifts.

What a sight it must be for a little child to walk into a sanctuary and to encounter a forty-foot "singing" Christmas tree, decorated with the radiant faces of our choir members whose voices resound from its branches! And around the tree, ten thousand beautifully wrapped presents shimmering

1

and shining, ready to be opened by eager hands! At the sight of this spectacle one small girl, breathless with awe, whispered to the woman next to her, "Am I in heaven?"

Our bus pastors know they must be sensitive to the needs of the boys and girls who travel to our church during the holiday festivities, because the children's lives at home may not reflect the joy of Christ's birth. On the way to receive his gift and to hear the story of Jesus, one little guy from a poor neighborhood shyly asked his bus pastor if he would pray with him.

"Of course I'll pray with you, son. What's the problem?"

"I want to ask God for an electric train," he explained.

The bus pastor was stuck. On the one hand, he was afraid that if the boy prayed for a train and didn't get it, his tender faith might be harmed. On the other hand, he wanted to encourage the child in his desire to pray. So he simply prayed, "Lord, if You want this boy to have an electric train, we ask You to make it happen. If You have a reason to say *no* to his request, he will understand that You are wise and know what is best for him. Your will be done, Lord. But he'd really like to have an electric train."

The bus pastor, a little uncomfortable about the situation, didn't tell a soul about the boy or his prayer. However, his heart was touched and troubled, so he continued to ask God to intercede—somehow.

Standing in the back of the church, the little boy stared wide-eyed at the incredible mountain of gifts. Wondering which package would be his, he waited his turn. Finally he went to the front to accept his gift, and a large, heavy package was handed to him. Trembling with excitement, he ripped off the paper. To his astonishment, the brand new electric train he had dreamed about and prayed for was right there in his hands!

Of all the thousands of families that donated gifts that year, one family had felt led to buy a complete Lionel electric train set, tracks and all. It had been placed with thousands of other gifts beside the tree. And that one gift—selected for him by the most random chance—was the gift the little boy received.

"God gave me my train," the boy told the bus pastor matter-of-factly as he boarded the bus to go home. The driver did a double take and then breathed a prayer of thanks. Never before had he been so keenly aware that our God is able to do "exceeding abundantly above all that we ask or think" (Eph. 3:20).

A Cabbage Patch Dream

ANOTHER CHRISTMAS. ANOTHER CHILD. ANOTHER DREAM. Tracy, one of the little girls in our church, lost her mother, Lynn, just weeks before Christmas. After the funeral, Tracy went to live with her Grandma Carol. Many of our church people had heavy hearts, thinking about the pain the little girl must be feeling. They dreamed of finding some special way to help her feel the love of Jesus, even though her mother had been taken from her so tragically. But how?

One adult Sunday school class had collected more than a hundred children's Christmas presents for our gift program that year, and one of those presents was a Cabbage Patch baby doll. For some reason, the woman responsible for the gifts put the doll aside and didn't place it under our tree with the other festively wrapped packages. She felt sure that someone special was supposed to have it, although at the time she had no idea who that someone would be.

Just before Christmas, the woman and her husband went

to visit the little girl and her Grandma Carol. On impulse, the woman pulled the Cabbage Patch doll out of the closet and took it along. She explained to her husband, "I think we should give the doll to Tracy. It's a beautiful gift, and it will cheer her up. Can you imagine a child losing her mother at this time of year?"

When the doll was presented to Tracy, she beamed with pleasure, hugging it tightly. Every little girl knows that Cabbage Patch dolls come with a unique name given to them by the manufacturer, so she asked the obvious question, "What's her name?"

The woman's husband read the Cabbage Patch name tag aloud: "It says her name is Lynnette Carol."

As if she couldn't believe her ears, the girl asked again, "What's her name?"

"Lynnette Carol," the man repeated.

The room fell silent, and the man and his wife looked at each other, momentarily bewildered. Then Grandma Carol, with tears in her eyes, explained to her grandchild, "This doll was meant for you, honey. Your mommy's name was Lynn, and my name is Carol. I think Lynnette Carol is Jesus' way of letting you know that He loves you very much, don't you?"

Dreams of Glory

Like most young boys I had some dreams of glory, and they centered on athletic competition. I loved sports, and with all my heart I longed to excel at them. But there was one problem: I was very small for my age. Thinking I could make up for my size with determination and courage, I tried out for the school football team.

"Son," said the football coach, shaking his head, "you've got some talent, but you're way too small. This is a rough, mean sport, and at your size, you'll get hurt. I'm sorry, but I can't let you play."

Next to football, my second choice was basketball. Of course I knew I was short, but I had a great shot, and I was a hustler. So I tried out.

"Son," the basketball coach smiled, "I admire your speed, and you've got some talent. But you're not tall enough to play basketball in this league. Maybe in a year or two..."

I was frustrated, but I wasn't going to give up. If I

couldn't excel at sports, I would excel at academics. I began to study more, to work harder than I'd ever worked before. I was smart, and I was focused. But when the National Honor Society test results came back, I had missed the cut by one percentage point.

Since I'd grown up in church, I knew that serving God was more important than anything. One night I listened as the congregation applauded when a star basketball player committed his future to God. Another young man, a star baseball pitcher, told the church that he was giving up baseball to serve God full time. He got a standing ovation. Knowing God could use anybody, I stood up and announced that I was going to give my future to Him. One lady said, "Oh, my God!" Otherwise, there was no rejoicing.

Then I was invited to speak at a youth service. I stood up and preached, and at the end I gave an altar call. There was a boy in our group named Paul Snyder who had long refused to accept Christ. He stubbornly denied that Jesus was Lord, and everyone had tried for years to change his mind.

That night I watched in amazement as Paul Snyder came down the aisle, weeping and repentant.

When Paul got on his knees, rockets went off in my heart. I felt like God was saying something very important to me: "You may not be big enough for football. You may not be tall enough for basketball. You may not be smart enough for the National Honor Society. But if you can pull a soul out of hell, then you qualify for My work. You can rescue the perishing and care for the dying."

That day my dreams of glory came true. But there was one important difference—the glory went to God, not to Tommy Barnett.

Unafraid to Dream

WHEN MY MOTHER, JOY, WAS FIRST MARRIED TO MY FATHER, a young, energetic evangelist named Herschel Barnett, she was as quiet as her husband was outgoing. She was tremendously proud of him and prayed every day that God would bless his ministry. But my mother was busy caring for my sister and me, and she kept a low profile.

One hot Texas night Dad held a revival in a town called Olony. The meeting continued late into the night, and Joy slipped out of the sanctuary and returned to the guest room in the parsonage next door where she went to bed. Since there was no air conditioning, she left the window open so the cool breeze could drift into her upstairs room. She drifted in and out of sleep with a grateful spirit, delighted that Dad's preaching was bringing so many to Christ.

As she dozed, she was peacefully aware of the sounds of worshipers leaving the parking lot. Then, all at once, she was jarred awake by the clear voices of two men who were talking outside. Their words were so distinct the men might as well have been in the room with her.

"Well, what did you think of that young evangelist?" one of them asked.

"He's a good little preacher," replied the other. "I think he'll go a long way."

"But what about that wife of his? What's your impression of her? You know, she can't play the guitar or sing. In fact, from what I saw, she can't do much of anything!"

The conversation faded as the two men walked away. But Joy Barnett had heard all she needed to hear. She was devastated. How could she ever have dreamed that she would be a good preacher's wife? Of course she had no talent—she knew that herself. From what she'd just heard, she would never be anything but a millstone about her beloved husband's neck.

"Oh God, help me," she prayed, sliding onto her knees beside the bed. She began to weep. "Lord, isn't it enough that I love You with all my heart? I'm willing to follow You and endure hardship for You. Isn't that enough?"

She sobbed brokenly in the silence, then picked up her prayer again. "Lord, You know I don't have any talent, and You know that self-consciousness destroys my confidence. There's no way I'll ever be able to stand up in front of an audience. Lord, please help me! How can I be the right wife for my husband when I have so many limitations?"

When Herschel returned she was still wide awake, but she pretended she was sleeping so he wouldn't notice her tear-stained face. She prayed silently all night, and when morning light finally dawned, she knew what she had to do. She remembered the story of Moses, who also thought he had nothing to offer God.

"What is that in thine hand?" God had asked him (Exod. 4:2).

What did Joy Barnett have in her hand?

She began to inventory the things she could do: She had artistic ability. She was gifted at writing dramatic scripts. She could design costumes and paint sets. She weighed the idea of taking guitar lessons and learning to sing.

But the most important gift my mother had was her faith. By the time that terrible night was over she knew that God would work through her, helping her to fulfill her dreams, enabling her to do what she couldn't accomplish in her own strength.

She became an outstanding pastor's wife—partners together with her husband in one of the denomination's largest churches. She was a terrific counselor, drama and choir director, teacher, and much sought-after public speaker.

Years later my mother wrote of the incident: "The outcome? Complete reliance on the Lord who gave me the courage to do the thing I was afraid to do, which was the only way to overcome. I would rather be dead than bound by fear. 'For God hath not given us the spirit of fear; but of power, and of love, and of a sound mind'" (2 Tim. 1:7).

A Packrat's Dream

As a pastor, my father had a passion for the elderly folks who found it hard to get to church on Sunday mornings. After a bout with illness, one old lady who had ridden the bus to church for years was no longer able to get herself to the bus. Dad asked a gentleman in the congregation to pick her up in a car and drive her to church.

"But, Pastor, she's on one of our bus routes," the man complained. "Why do we have to pick her up in a car?"

"I don't ask people to do anything I wouldn't do myself," Dad patiently explained. "She needs to get to church—it's the only contact with Christian people she has, and if she wants to worship, we need to make sure she can. If she can't manage to ride the bus anymore, then she needs to be helped to a car and driven to church. I'd really appreciate it if you'd help me out with this."

Reluctant but faithful, the man did as he was asked and stopped every Sunday at the woman's run-down house. He helped her get in the car, into the church, and back again.

Now this wasn't the cleanest little lady in the world. She didn't dress especially well, and she didn't smell especially good. When a visitation team showed up at her door one day, they watched in dismay as rats and insects scurried among the newspapers that were piled halfway to the ceiling in every room. She was a packrat who hadn't cleaned her house for decades.

One day the phone rang at Dad's house, and he was told that the old woman had died of an unexpected heart attack. The funeral was, to say the least, not well-attended. But a few days later, Dad received an unexpected phone call from the relative who was executing her will.

The old lady who had lived in poverty, surrounded by her newspapers and rodents and roaches, had cherished a dream in her heart: She wanted to do something special for Dad's church when she died. She was grateful. She had been blessed. And she hadn't been as poor as she looked, either. In her will she left the church eighty thousand dollars. In those days that generous gift was able to purchase eight brand-new church buses! Her dream was fulfilled—and because of her generosity, so were the dreams of many others.

A Family of Dreamers

BEFORE MOVING TO PHOENIX I PASTORED A CHURCH IN Davenport, Iowa, which experienced explosive growth in just a couple of years. During my first year as pastor, it went from seventy-six people to five hundred. The next year it had grown to two thousand. It was a wonderful blessing, but I found myself working from daybreak till dinner, then returning to church until ten o'clock at night. I was the preacher, the music minister, the marriage counselor, the janitor, and, when we began to construct a larger sanctuary, I was also the building contractor.

My boys were very young then—Matthew was four and Luke was eight. One night they said, "Dad, are you going to stay home with us tonight? We sure miss being with you."

I looked at them sadly. "No," I shook my head. "I really wish I could stay home, but I've got a board meeting."

"We don't get to see you anymore, Dad. Can't we come to the board meeting? At least we'd be able to ride with you."

13

I was both touched and grieved by their request. Of course I said yes. And with great joy, the two of them piled into the car with me, chattering happily all the way to church. They shot baskets while the meeting went on . . . and on . . . and on. By the time every conceivable church concern had been settled, hours had passed. I looked at my watch; it was after eleven o'clock. I opened the door to leave, and there were Matthew and Luke, covered up in choir robes, sound asleep. Their little blond heads were pressed against the door, as close to me as they could get. My heart broke.

I carried them, one after the other, to the car. I placed Matthew in the back seat, and Luke in the front, his head on my knee. "Lord," I prayed as I drove home, "I don't want to save the world and lose these boys. I wish I had more time to spend with them."

I carried Matthew upstairs to his bed and then carried Luke to his. Just as I tucked Luke in, his blue eyes opened wide. "Thanks for letting me be with you tonight, Dad. I'd rather be with you than with anybody in the whole world!"

That's all it took. Tears poured down my face. "Son, I'd rather be with you and Matthew and Kristie and your mother than anyone else, too. My being away from you isn't a way of saying I don't love you. God has given me the most wonderful family in the world. In fact, I want to pray right now and give you back to Him."

I gently laid my hands on Luke's tousled hair and prayed, "Lord, I've given everything to You, but I haven't completely given You this boy. I give him to You now."

As I finished, I heard a little voice. "Dear God, You know how much my dad means to me. Being with him is so important to me. But now I want to give my dad to You, too."

How I wept as my son and I committed each other to God! And God heard our prayers. Within days, a turn of events at the church made it possible for me to be with my family nearly every night. I gave my children to Him, and He gave them back to me. Today, all three of them are still wholeheartedly His, still walking with Him, still serving Him—for me, a dream come true.

The Dream Chair

FOR FIVE YEARS, G. G. HAD BEEN RIDING TO PHOENIX FIRST Assembly in one of our wheelchair-access buses. She was a devoted Christian, a faithful intercessor, always willing to help, especially with our greeting card correspondence. Never in good health, in one year her condition went from bad to worse.

G. G. suffered from cystic fibrosis, which affected her lungs and made it very difficult for her to breathe. Now she had reached the point where it was necessary for her to be placed on oxygen twenty-four hours a day. This made breathing easier and relieved some of the severe strain on her heart. But her condition continued to deteriorate, and it became increasingly difficult for G. G. to get to church. Everyone missed her, and many in our church family wanted to know what they could do to help. Sadly, there didn't seem to be much anybody could do except pray.

Christmas was approaching, and one of our women's ministry leaders went to visit G. G. at the low-income residence where she lived. The woman explained that our "Christmas for Jesus" ministry gave families the opportunity to bless others in the church who had specific needs, and she asked G. G. what particular needs she had.

There was a long pause. "I honestly don't have any needs," G. G. smiled. "I really have everything I need."

The woman tried a different approach. "Is there a special desire of your heart that you don't really think you *need,* but you'd enjoy anyway?"

G. G. thought for a moment and smiled again. "You know, it would be nice to have a Lazy Boy-type recliner. It would make it easier for me to breathe. But really, that's asking way too much. There are so many other people out there with greater needs than that."

The woman was almost speechless. Breathing was about as great a need as she could imagine! She gently told G. G., "We'll leave that up to the Lord, because with Him nothing is too difficult." And as she drove away from G. G.'s modest home, she began to get excited. *Wouldn't it be neat if God provided that chair?* she thought as she filled out a prayer request form.

Not many days later, a family called the church. They had intended to sell some furniture, but God had impressed it upon their hearts that they should give it away. Would the church be interested? Sure enough, in the collection of unwanted furniture—all of which was in excellent condition—there was not just one but *two* recliner chairs.

On December 23, the family delivered the chair to G. G. and added a basket of fruit and other goodies. "This is the most wonderful Christmas I've ever had!" G. G. exulted, stunned to see her dream chair sitting right there in her room. It was also G. G.'s last Christmas on this earth. She went home to be with the Lord early the following year in the fulfillment of her greatest dreams of all: to see the face of her beloved Savior.

One Dream Leads to Another

ONE OF THE WONDERFUL THINGS ABOUT GOD'S GIFTS IS THAT they are never completely unwrapped. They keep unfolding, decade after decade, from one generation to the next.

When I was pastoring in Davenport, winter came while we were in the midst of a major building project. The temperature was around zero degrees, and we simply didn't have enough volunteers to finish the building. I was working with hammer and nails myself, day in and day out, praying that God would send us workers. I was tired—more tired than I could ever remember being. There weren't enough hours in the day for me to accomplish everything I needed to do.

One day I received a phone call from Mrs. Derry. She was at the end of her rope. Her children had come to our church as part of our bus ministry, and eventually she too had accepted Jesus Christ as her Savior.

"Are you married?" I asked, wondering why she called.

"Oh, yes. But…"

I breathed a quick prayer. "Tell me about your husband. Is he a Christian man?"

"Are you kidding? Look, Pastor, to be perfectly honest, my husband, Phil, is a hopeless alcoholic. And we are in desperate straits financially because he drinks away every paycheck he earns." Her dreams of a happy family were drowning in a river of alcohol.

I listened rather sadly to a story of addiction and devastation that repeats itself again and again in families across the world. When she finished, I asked, "How can I help?"

She paused for a moment and replied, "I think the only way you can help is by leading Phil to Jesus. Only God can save our marriage."

Of course she was right, so I went to the family home to talk to him. Sometimes visits like that are futile and end in disappointment. But fortunately, Phil was ready for a change himself. After we talked awhile, he humbled himself, confessed his sins before God, and invited Jesus to come into his life. He received the gift of salvation—but God's gift-giving had only just begun.

Almost immediately, Phil Derry's wife began to see her dreams restored. And at about the same time, I received a blessing, too. Phil Derry wanted to help with the construction work at the church. He worked long and hard and made my job far easier. Then he had another idea.

"I want to be a bus pastor," he confided one day.

Phil started with one bus, and soon it was filled with kids. Before long he had filled four more buses. Unsatisfied with his Sunday route, he started another one on Saturdays. Soon fifteen hundred children were attending church every Saturday, hearing the good news about Jesus' love.

Eventually Phil and his family moved to California, where he started a church of his own in the Los Angeles' area. With his usual commitment to kids, he quickly built

19

up another bus ministry that brought in dozens of boys and girls to hear the gospel message. That bus ministry reached into the heart of the city, and countless kids received the gift of salvation. Those young people might never have heard about Jesus' personal love for them if it hadn't been for Phil Derry's faithfulness.

One of the many children Phil reached out to was a thirteen-year-old boy named Julian Torrez. And because of the way God's gifts continue to unfold, Julian Torrez is now the bus pastor at our Dream Center in Los Angeles. He, like Phil before him, is carrying God's love into the city on a fleet of buses. Today he oversees the transport and Christian education of four thousand children in L.A.'s inner city.

Years ago, Phil Derry received the gift of salvation. Through him, thousands of children have met—and continue to meet—the Giver of every good and perfect gift.

A Dream to Minister

LEO WAS A MAN WITH A BIG DREAM. THE SON OF A POLISH emigrant family, he attended our church in Phoenix, and on more than one occasion, he told me that he wanted to serve on my pastoral staff. Now, at the time I didn't know Leo well, so my immediate reaction to his dream could be summed up in two words: *No way.*

But Leo's outspoken desire to minister had caught my attention, and so I began to observe him. Every Sunday, week after week, I saw him sitting in the second row of the sanctuary, carefully dressed in a suit and tie. I was also aware that he had become faithful in his tithing—which told me that when it came to a Christian commitment, he wasn't just pretending.

One Sunday, Leo grabbed me by the arm and said, "How would you like to preach to three thousand French people this summer?"

I stared at him skeptically. "Well, of course I'd like to, but

I'm not going to France, so that seems rather unlikely."

"No, you don't understand, Pastor. I mean how would you like to preach to three thousand French people right here in Phoenix, in this church?"

"Sounds great, Leo." That's what I *said*. What I thought was, *This guy is nuts.* There probably isn't one French person in the entire city of Phoenix.

As the days and weeks passed the conversation faded in my mind, and I only remembered it when I noticed Leo sitting in the second row every Sunday, meticulously dressed, listening intently to my message.

One summer Saturday at 11:00 P.M., as I was putting my finishing touches on the next day's sermon, my phone rang. I quickly answered it, wondering what kind of emergency might have taken place. But it wasn't an emergency, at least not exactly. It was Leo. "Tomorrow's the day, Pastor!" he announced cheerfully.

I rubbed my eyes and replied, "Tomorrow is *what* day, Leo?"

"Tomorrow is the day that the French people are coming to church! I'm sorry, but I could only get two thousand French people. Oh, and by the way, they don't speak English, so we'll need an interpreter. See you tomorrow, Pastor."

I hung up the phone, shaking my head. I still didn't quite believe him.

The next morning I was in the church office when one of the greeters rushed in from the sanctuary, having literally run across the parking lot. "Pastor! What are we going to do? We've got the strangest people coming into the service. They're either speaking in tongues, or we're going to need an interpreter."

I quickly arranged for someone to interpret my sermon into French, and before the morning was over, I found myself addressing two thousand French people, just as Leo had promised. Later he explained that his brothers headed up a multilevel marketing company in France, and they had brought their best sales personnel to the United States as a reward for top performance. Leo had somehow managed to bring every last one of them to church!

As it turned out, sixteen hundred of those visitors came forward at the end of the service to accept Jesus Christ as their Savior. And, with irrepressible enthusiasm, Leo baptized five hundred of them in the church fountain after the morning worship service.

I probably don't have to tell you the rest: Later on that week I hired a new staff member. Today, Leo Godzich is responsible for our church's marriage ministry and teaches a Sunday school class with more than four hundred in attendance. He is such a key part of our ministry team that I honestly don't know what we did without him.

Leo had a dream, all right. And despite my doubts—and with a little help from the Lord—his dream came true.

Dreams and Dedication

FRED, A VOLUNTEER IN OUR VISITATION MINISTRY, IS A MAN who believes in dreams, but he also understands a very important principle: Dreams are most likely to come true when people are dedicated and faithful to whatever the Lord gives them to do.

After hearing me speak about dreams on television, a woman from California wrote to me. She told me that she'd had several dreams, and she was believing God for my help with one of them. "My stepson in Phoenix has AIDS," she explained in her letter, "and he has no friends and family there. He is quite sick—his weight has dropped to one hundred three pounds, and he is lonely and depressed. He needs a kind word from someone who isn't paid to be nice to him. He really needs encouragement. But most of all he needs to be born again. His name is David."

Our visitation ministry gave the letter to Fred and asked him to follow up. Fred left several messages on the young man's answering machine. After receiving no response, he figured he'd try the following Saturday to make personal contact with him. When Fred arrived at the apartment complex where David lived, the neighbors told him he was too late. "He was taken away in an ambulance this morning with internal bleeding," they said.

Fred's frustration was only exceeded by his determination to track down this very sick young man. After finding out which hospital David had been taken to, he called to see if there was anything he could do to help. "There's really not much anyone can do," a hospital employee told him. So he headed home.

But while Fred was driving toward his house, God began to reveal to him just how much He loved David. Fred began to understand that if David had been the only man on earth, Jesus would have died for his sins. Tears flooded his eyes. No matter what the hospital had said, he knew he hadn't done quite enough for David.

"Okay, God," Fred prayed as he turned his car around and headed for the hospital. "You make a way for me to get in to see him, and please—open his heart to Your truth." As he drove, Fred's mind wandered to some of the other things he could have been doing that day. *This is a probably a wild goose chase,* he fretted. But remembering God's love for David, Fred shut the distractions out and continued to pray.

When he walked into the hospital, he asked the information volunteer for help. He was sent to one nursing station, then another, then another. Finally a nurse found David's name on her computer screen. "Are you family?" she asked.

"No, I'm not, but . . ."

"Are you aware of his condition?"

"Yes. I know."

"You may be able to get in, but it will be a long wait." Fred seated himself in a waiting room and tried to occupy himself with prayer while the clock ticked off an hour and a half.

"You can come in now," a nurse finally told him, "but you'll have to wear a mask and gloves."

Fred was feeling more and more foolish. He thought he looked ridiculous in the mask, and besides, he didn't even know David. What on earth would he say once he got inside the room?

Fred cautiously entered David's room. "I'm Fred Post," he introduced himself. "I came to see you to let you know that our church is concerned about you. But most of all I want you to know that Jesus loves you. He wants to forgive your sins and come into your heart. Would you like to pray with me?"

To Fred's great relief, David was very open to his words. He willingly prayed for forgiveness and accepted Jesus. Then he told Fred about something that had puzzled him for some time. "I was in an AIDS hospice once, and everybody else who was in there died except for me. Why did I survive?"

Fred, in awe of God's persistent love for this young man, simply said, "I believe God spared you because He loves you so much that He wanted you to have this opportunity to accept Jesus."

Fred went back to see David the next day and found that the young man was much worse. "Jesus is with you," he reminded David, who weakly responded, "He is. He is."

"You belong to Jesus now, David. Keep your eyes on Him."

By now the frail young man could barely muster the strength to say, "You too..."

As Fred left, David somehow managed to call out, "Thank you." And that night, David went home to be with Jesus.

A Kitchen-Floor Dreamer

LARRY KERYCHUK PLAYED QUARTERBACK AT IDAHO STATE, and after a great college career, he went on to play for the Canadian Football League's Edmonton Eskimos. When he finally retired from football he came to our church. In fact, the very first week I was in Phoenix Larry sat on my kitchen floor and said, "I've got a dream to start a ministry to athletes. Hundreds of athletes would come and spend three days learning about the Christian life. Eventually we would develop an Olympic village with a gymnasium, a swimming pool, a track, and a weight room so that athletes could come from all over the world to train for the Olympics and go through our discipleship program."

It was a dynamic dream but not a very practical one. In those early days in Phoenix our church had some very basic groundwork to lay, and there was no time or money for extravagant ideas—even soul-stirring ones like Larry's.

Still, I wanted to get Larry involved in ministry. As I

looked out over the congregation each Sunday, I couldn't help but notice him—he was such an outstanding young man. I finally asked him if he would be a youth pastor. He agreed, knowing that the Lord had called him into *some* sort of Christian outreach.

He did okay, but the youth ministry sort of sputtered along. Then Larry began to do two things: He started to systematically memorize Scripture and to pray an hour or two every morning in the church. And as he put those spiritual disciplines to work in his life, a dream emerged in Larry's heart that changed our church forever.

Larry explained his idea to me: "Other churches and organizations want their young people to commit two years of their lives for ministry, but I'd like to ask young people to give just one year of their life to full-time Christian service. During that year they'll start at seven in the morning and spend their first hour on the mountainside in prayer. Between eight and nine, they'll memorize Scriptures— they'll have to memorize six hundred Scriptures during the year to graduate. They'll attend Bible study the next hour, then they'll eat. Then they'll go out and minister on the streets in various ways."

I was blown away by Larry's dream. We called the new program "The Master's Commission." It exploded! Today, young people from across the globe are receiving top-notch discipleship training at the various Master's Commission locations around the world.

But Larry wasn't finished. He walked into my office one day and said, "I've been thinking about starting something else." And at last we began to revisit his original dream of three-day athletic conferences.

Once the conferences got underway, more and more athletes attended each year. Eventually, more than seven hundred of the greatest sports figures in America were joining us, focusing their attention on the things of the

Lord. Great men of God like Evander Holyfield, David Robinson, and Barry Sanders shared their faith and listened to rich spiritual teaching. Then athletes began to arrive from all around the world. It was at one of these conferences that the Holy Spirit touched Colorado football coach Bill McCartney, inspiring him to make his Promise Keepers dream a reality.

Larry quietly persevered, warmed by the success of his athletic conferences. But in his heart he had also kept alive the dream of a Christian Olympic village. Now it is no longer a dream. A man recently gave Larry two and one-half million dollars, with a promise of another ten million dollars, to build a great Olympic-training site. The first building is under construction. Larry Kerychuk's kitchen-floor dream is finally becoming a reality—and it is changing the hearts of gifted young athletes in the United States and beyond.

Dreams and Networking

THE BIBLE SAYS THAT ONE SHALL PUT A THOUSAND TO FLIGHT and two shall put ten thousand to flight (Deut. 32:30). In others words, when it comes to God's work, there is a unique kind of multiplication that takes place. Today, when we dream of changing the world with the gospel, we need to look for ways to multiply our impact. One of the best ways, I believe, is through networking.

When my son Matthew and I first went to Los Angeles to establish a church, we had no idea how to reach that huge and diverse city. Neither of us had any experience in cross-cultural evangelism—yet never before had we seen so many cultures all within the limits of a single, sprawling metropolis. Over the years the churches I'd pastored had given millions of dollars to foreign missions work. But the truth is, we had neglected our home field. And now, although our hands and hearts were willing to do whatever we could, we didn't know where to begin.

The inner-city people saw Matthew's blond, clean-cut good looks and asked, "Are you a Mormon?"

They looked at me and saw a fifty-six-year-old white man with no rhythm.

There we were, two white guys—one barely out of his teens, the other nearing senior citizenship. Together we had a dream of reaching the inner city with the gospel. But how? Ideas and programs from Phoenix simply didn't work in L.A. So after getting nowhere for a while, we decided, "Let's reach out to the ministers who are already succeeding."

We put out the word: "Come and help us!" And God sent the right people.

We met some folks who had a motorcycle ministry and offered them a place to hold services in the "Dream Center"—the old Queen of the Angels Hospital that we were refurbishing. We met a young man who had sidewalk Sunday school trailers but no ministry, so we bought the trailers. We met Clayton Gallagher who, for seventeen years, had ministered to runaway kids but had no place to house them—we gave him an entire floor of the old hospital. We met a man whose Friendship Ministry feeds 155,000 people a week.

"I'm going to give you food to help you get started," he said. He gave us truckloads of provisions to feed the hungry Angeleno families who came to us.

As we continued to seek help, we learned that many of the ethnic communities in Los Angeles didn't speak English. So we started a Russian church with a Russian pastor. We started a Chinese church with a Chinese pastor and a Cambodian church with a Cambodian pastor. We added a Filipino pastor, a Jewish pastor, a Brazilian, an Ethiopian, until we'd established eleven ethnic churches.

Today there are one hundred eighty ministries networking together at the Dream Center. Besides those ministries, we've been assisted by commercial enterprises like Guess? Jeans and communication networks such as TBN and Lifeline. The Dream Center ministers to fifteen thousand people a week, and we feed twenty-five thousand people a week. And we believe that by the year 2001 we'll be reaching one hundred thousand men, women, and children a year.

Through networking, and by God's grace, our dream for ministering in L.A. is coming true.

Nightmares and Dreams

MATTHEW WAS NOT THE FIRST PERSON I CONSIDERED TO serve as the pastor of our Dream Center in Los Angeles. But he was God's first choice, and my only concern about his work there today is that he never stops to rest. His enthusiasm is so wholehearted that I worry at times about his physical body being able to keep up with his powerfully motivated spirit.

But I'll never forget the feelings I experienced when I traveled with him to the Dream Center—and had to leave him there alone to begin his ministry. He was only twenty years old and had never pastored. How could I leave? What was he facing?

It was less than two hours after I left Matthew at the Dream Center that two gang members were shot, and one was killed on the street right in front of the church. Matthew was deeply shaken, and not knowing what else to do, he held the young man in his arms while he died. Later that day he talked to the heartbroken family and learned that they had no money for a funeral. With characteristic concern, he went back to the church, and the youth group Matthew met with for the first time took up an offering for the dead boy's family. The offering wasn't large, only thirty dollars, but it was given with love.

Feeling very vulnerable, Matthew found his way to the home of the slain gangster. When he arrived, the house was full of the dead man's "homeboys." With his blond hair and blue eyes, Matthew was clearly from a different world. But God had sent him, so he offered the small gift of money to the parents. The boy's mother embraced him tearfully. Then she turned on the other young men and began to scream at them: "Get out of here! It's your fault my boy is dead! Get out of here!"

Matthew was becoming extremely uncomfortable. Telling the distressed woman once again that he was terribly sorry about her son's death and moving toward the front door, he felt a hand firmly grip his shoulder. *I'm going to be assaulted,* he thought. In that highly charged emotional situation, what else could he expect?

Matthew turned around, and the young Mexican man standing nearest him quietly said, "Will you pray with us before you go?"

Matthew glanced around the room in disbelief. But there they all stood, waiting for him to pray. One by one they joined hands with Matthew, and he began to pray with all his heart for the family, the young men, and the neighborhood. As he finished his prayer, the gang members, hands still clasped, raised their arms—and Matthew's—high above their heads, a sign that he was now considered one of them.

In the months that followed this incident, Matthew led many of these same young men to the Lord.

California Dreaming

WHAT DO GANGSTERS DREAM ABOUT? WHAT DO THEY LONG for? What appeals to them *before* they get involved in their violent, destructive lifestyles? From what we know, at first they want to feel like they belong to somebody, to something, to some group where they fit in and feel at home. Many of them come from disintegrated families, and their fellow "homeboys" are the only family they have. Then, once the group culture of violence empowers them, they often move on to dreams of money, revenge, status, and control.

When we first established the Dream Center, the Temple Street Gang lived across the street from our facility. We found ourselves in the midst of an ongoing battle against their graffiti, their harassment of girls and women at the center, and threats against our work. Meanwhile, we learned that they were also pursuing crime and drug trafficking throughout the surrounding neighborhood.

For several months our team attempted to reach out to these young men, who numbered around fifteen, but they were hard as nails; they refused to give us the time of day. Finally, one Easter morning, some of the courageous members of the center's Hope for Homeless Youth confronted them and all but physically propelled them into our Easter service. The gang members were Hispanic, and they respected the sacredness of Easter. So there they were, dressed in their gangster garb, sitting in our church.

If there was anything those young men could relate to, it was physical violence, bloodshed, and death. My son Matthew preached powerfully that morning, and as he described the brutal death Jesus suffered on the cross for the sins of every person there, the Holy Spirit began to move within the hearts of the Temple Street gangsters. By the end of his sermon, Matthew had the clear impression that three of these young men would come to Christ.

At first, Matthew asked those who wanted to acknowledge that Jesus Christ had died for their sins to raise their hands. Among others, three hands were instantly raised. Minutes later three hardened young men rushed to the front of the chapel, tears pouring down their faces. They were immediately surrounded by a group of young believers, some of whom had left their own gangs to live at the Dream Center. In the company of others so like themselves, they recited the sinner's prayer and wept as Jesus forgave their sins and came into their lives.

That same day they were baptized in the Pacific Ocean, coming up out of the water with shouts of joy and victory. From that day on, those ex-gangsters entered a discipleship program, began to study God's Word, and committed themselves to reaching out to others who are snared in the deadly trap of gang life—with its drugs, alcohol, drive-by shootings, and vengeance.

In less than a day, three members of the Temple Street

Gang found a new dream. Through the forgiveness and love of Jesus Christ, they have come home to a place of belonging where love reigns, where power comes from God, and where a wealth of spiritual treasure is theirs for the asking.

A Dream of True Love

LIKE MOST YOUNG GIRLS, CARLA DREAMED OF BEING LOVED. But her need for love was desperate, and it seemed to her that it would never be met. She never knew her mother, who had left her tiny daughter behind in her own pursuit of drugs and prostitution. And it wasn't long after her mother's departure that Carla's dream of love was eclipsed by her determination to escape family abuse. Fleeing domestic violence, she ran away from home and hit the streets of Hollywood. Carla was barely fourteen when she found herself following in her mother's tragic footsteps.

One night, Carla walked into a local nightclub looking for a good time. There she met a man who seemed to want to make her dream of being loved come true. He said she was beautiful. He promised to give her everything she had ever wanted. He took her to his home, whispering the sweet words of romance she'd always wanted to hear. He bought her new clothes and told her how to wear her hair.

The man also filled Carla's young body with cocaine. The cocaine was free, and there was so much of it that she was almost immediately addicted. Carla had no way of knowing that the man was a pimp. Nor did she imagine that he had intentionally hooked her on cocaine so she would sell her body to satisfy her craving. But it wasn't long before Carla found out what was on her lover's mind. And sad to say, it wasn't love.

During those terrible days, Carla got pregnant and gave birth to her only child. She loved that baby the minute she saw him. Although drugs had wreaked havoc on her mind, some part of her still felt a deep love for her newborn child. But a "friend" who was living with her became annoyed because the baby wouldn't stop crying. Growing more and more enraged, he finally pulled out a gun and shot the infant in the head four times. Carla's child was murdered in cold blood as she watched helplessly.

Carla's heart was broken. Although she was almost unable to function, her pimp was merciless. He demanded that she return to the streets as a prostitute, threatening to kill her if she didn't. He put a gun in her mouth to make sure she knew he meant business. He resorted to unspeakable forms of torture in his efforts to control her. In one horrible scene, he assaulted her with a hot curling iron, and the injuries she sustained have made it impossible for her to bear another child.

One Monday night while she walked aimlessly around the streets of Hollywood, Carla heard the strains of music. It sounded like a live band, so she made her way over to a small gathering of people. She was surprised to see a street outreach from the Dream Center, but her curiosity drew her closer. *Who were these people? Was this some kind of a trap?* She stayed in the shadows, feeling vaguely suspicious of their motives. But as she listened to a clear and honest message about God's love, about His forgiveness, about His ability to turn lives around, Carla found her way to the front. She prayed with a street minister—and, quite unexpectedly, her dream of love stirred within her once again.

That night, Carla was rescued from the streets of Hollywood. She was given a place to live and was put through a detox program, which, with God's help, has set her free from her addictions. Best of all, Carla has been warmly embraced by a community of Christians who have loved her, taught her the truths of the Bible, and have given her back the future she had so brutally lost. Today Carla lives at the Dream Center, where her dreams of true love—*real* love, God's *unconditional love*—have finally come true.

A Dream Family

AN OUTREACH TEAM MET GEORGE ON ONE OF L.A.'S MEANEST streets. George was hanging out with a group of tough-looking young men who seemed at first glance like the most unlikely candidates for Christian conversion. After taking one good look at them, most of us would have felt like walking away. But the teams that go out from the Dream Center aren't easily intimidated. Many of them have come off the streets themselves. That night they courageously told George and the others about Jesus and invited them to a Wednesday night prayer service at the Dream Center.

Sometimes the toughest appearances hide the tenderest hearts. George had always wanted to belong to a family, and the family of God was suddenly inviting him to join them. He was only too happy to repent, seek forgiveness for his sins, and receive Jesus Christ into his life. At the invitation, he hurried forward, overjoyed at the promise of forgiveness and a new beginning. In the weeks that followed it wasn't difficult to build a relationship with George—in fact, nothing could keep him away from church activities.

Our team didn't know much about George's background, but that wasn't unusual. Many of the youth who come to the Lord at the Dream Center are from shattered families, and George was no exception. But to their surprise, the team discovered that although George's mother had returned to South America, his father wasn't missing. The good news was that his father was part of a Dream Center outreach. The bad news was that, apart from a miracle, he wasn't going to live much longer. He was one of the AIDS patients who were earnestly being taught about Jesus before embarking on their homeward journey.

One day George heard that his father was attending a service in the gym. With tears in his eyes, he ran across the campus to his father's side. Together, the two men stood in praise and worship before their newfound heavenly Father. George's dreams were coming true, but what would happen when his father died? Where would he go?

Because of his deep commitment to Christ and his extraordinary situation, the people at the Dream Center decided to adopt George as their own. They began to raise money and helped him enroll in the center's Christian school. Today George's future is in the hands of God, tended by his Christian family. George is part of the new generation of L.A. youth that God is raising up to carry the gospel into the new millennium. George's dad died a few days ago, and Matthew conducted his funeral at the Dream Center.

An Old Man's Dream

WHEN I WAS A YOUNG EVANGELIST I TOOK MY TENT TO Abilene, Kansas, and with the help of some local boys, I proceeded to set it up on a scorching summer day. Together we unfolded the heavy canvas and unpacked the ropes, pegs, and mallets. As we worked, we were interrupted by a raspy voice: "What's this all about?"

I turned and saw a ragged old man staring at us. "I'm having a revival meeting here tonight," I explained, "and I'd like to invite you to come."

The old man continued to stare. He had a deep scowl on his face, and I couldn't help but notice how severely he was bent over. He looked as if he were crouching, about to spring at us. The boys and I glanced at each other and kept on working.

"Just one more of them preachers come to town to take our money," he grumbled, shuffling off in disgust.

That night at our first meeting the old man showed up

with his wife. She tried to lead him forward to sit near the front; he refused to sit anywhere but in the back row.

The local pastor who was sponsoring the revival pointed him out to me. "If you could do anything with that old boy, it'd almost be worth the time you spend here," he said.

"Is he really that bad?"

"Worse than bad. He's the town agnostic, and he thinks nothing of drinking himself unconscious. He's out of touch with God and everybody else, including himself. If anybody ever fit the category of 'old reprobate,' he does."

The meeting hadn't even started and the old man was already griping—and he wasn't doing it quietly. I began to play my accordion and sing, unable to ignore the fact that most of the seats in the tent were empty, with only a handful of people clustered in the front. I welcomed everybody, played softly, and sang some familiar gospel songs. I noticed that the old man was having trouble hearing, irritably cupping his hand around his ear and leaning forward.

I began to sing and speak more softly.

The old man couldn't stand it. He got up and all but dragged his wife down to the front row where he crossed his arms and slumped in his seat. I noticed out of the corner of my eye that the local preacher had his eyes closed, praying. I was glad to see it.

I began my sermon, suddenly aware that the little handful of souls in front of me was at that moment the most important crowd in all the world. I preached my heart out, and at the end I appealed to them to ask God for forgiveness and come to Jesus for salvation. "One of His 'prodigal sons' is here in this town tonight. Maybe it is one of you. If it is, then listen to me, because He sent me to tell you to come home. He wants me to lead you back to Him."

I stepped down in front of the pulpit. "Which one of you is it? Come, take my hand right now."

I glanced at the old man, and I could hardly believe my

eyes. Tears were pouring down his stubbly gray beard. I looked directly at him. "He wants you to come home tonight. You've been away a long time, and it's been a tough road. But you're heading home tonight."

I began to sing *Just As I Am*. The old man got up, and with his wife's help, he shuffled up to me. He was sobbing so deeply that his entire body shook. We prayed with him for a long time, and when he left to go home, I had to look at him twice to believe my eyes. He was standing straight and tall. I still remember thinking that he didn't resemble the same old man very much at all.

That was the last night our meetings had a small turnout. That old man was the best advertisement for a revival that I've ever seen. He came early every day, clean-shaven and erect. And he brought the whole town with him.

When I left town he shook my hand, and I realized that I hadn't noticed how tall he was—he must have stood six foot six. "Son," he said, tears filling his eyes, "if you hadn't obeyed the voice of God and come to Abilene, this old man would have died without knowing that the Lord still wanted him to come home. I always dreamed that He still loved me, but somehow I just couldn't believe it. Not until you told me so."

A Difficult Dreamer

I GET LOTS OF MAIL, AND SOME OF THE LETTERS I RECEIVE
lift my heart and thrill my soul. I look forward to reading
the testimonies of women and men, girls and boys who
write to me about the way their lives have been changed
through our church's various ministries.

But when I opened *that* letter, I wouldn't say my heart
was lifted or my soul thrilled. Instead, I felt saddened and
deeply troubled. At the time I was unable to see that the
person who wrote it had a very specific dream well hidden
between the lines. I read her angry words once, then read
them again.

> Dear Pastor Barnett,
>
> After seeing you on television I decided to visit
> your church. All my life I've been disappointed by
> preachers and churches. For some reason I thought
> your church would be different. Instead, I was in for

yet another disappointment.

The music was too fast and too loud. The sermon was too fast and too loud. I couldn't get out of the building quickly enough!

As I left, I noticed that you had a section designated for wheelchairs. I figured those poor people wanted to get out of there as badly as I did, but they all had to wait their turn. I offered to help, but the people in charge refused to let me. I was insulted!

I wish I could say something nice about your church, but I can't. I just want you to know the truth and how disappointed I was.

The woman signed her name and wrote her address underneath. I stared at the harsh words, feeling immediately defensive. I wanted to write back and explain that our wheelchair-bound members—we affectionately call them the "Holy Rollers"—are covered by special insurance, which allows only certain workers to move them in and out of the sanctuary. I wanted to explain the purpose of our music and to enlighten her about preaching styles. My desire to explain quickly flared up in my spirit into a full-fledged attack of righteous indignation. *Who did she think she was, anyway?*

Fortunately, I've learned a few things over the years. And one of the most important lessons I've learned is that when I'm incensed, I'd better cool off before responding. I waited two days, and during that time the Lord began to show me what He knew the woman *needed*—which was a far cry from what I thought the woman *deserved*.

My dear friend,

Forgive me for disappointing you when you visited our church. I'm sorry the music was too loud and too fast. And as far as my sermon was concerned, your criticism of me was valid. I often go home after preaching and feel like a total failure, wondering if I should quit and turn over the church to somebody else. My raspy voice is not the best for preaching, and your letter has reminded me that it may be time for me to step down and turn the job over to somebody else.

As honestly as possible I humbled myself before the woman and took full responsibility for her disappointment. Then, before mailing the letter, I went out and purchased the most expensive Bible I could find and had the woman's name engraved on it in gold. Inside I wrote, "Please accept this Bible as a token of my love." And I signed my name.

The next Wednesday, I noticed in the congregation a very attractive, beautifully dressed middle-aged woman. After the service I found myself face to face with her. I tried to place her in my memory, but I couldn't.

"I'm the lady!" she said. "I'm the lady! Would you please forgive me?"

I stared at her uncomprehendingly.

"I'm the lady," she insisted, "who wrote you the letter. And I'm so sorry. This Bible is the most wonderful gift I've ever received." At that point, I noticed the Bible I had bought. She was clutching it against her heart. "It is the most valuable thing I've ever owned. Preacher, will you forgive me?"

"Of course . . ." I began, but she wasn't finished.

"You see, I'm a bitter woman, and that letter came from my bitter heart."

By now she was weeping. "I've been unhappy in my relationship with my family, and I guess I've been dreaming of a place where I would be loved unconditionally. Your letter and your gift of the Bible have shown me that this is the place. Thank you for loving me even when I was unlovable."

That woman still attends our church, and she has become a good friend of mine. I often think about her dream of being loved, hidden between the lines of her letter. What would have happened if I'd given her the kind of answer that I thought she deserved?

God's Man—In Your Dreams!

ONE TERRIBLE NIGHT WHEN JOSE WAS NINE YEARS OLD, HE watched his father beat his mother nearly to death. His father was a drunk and a drug addict. As a young child, Jose hated the very smell of beer because of what alcohol did to his father and what his father in turn did to his mother. That particular night, Jose promised his mother that he would never be like his father—he would never drink or do drugs. "Drinking changes people," he told her, "and I hate it." He promised her with all his heart that he would be different. He would be a good man in a bad world. That was young Jose's dream.

But by the time Jose was eleven years old, he had started stealing his father's beer. And when his dad passed out drunk, Jose stole money from his wallet and bought "weed" with it. Cocaine entered his life at age fourteen, and by the time he went to prison at age eighteen, he had killed a rival gang member in a drive-by shooting.

For weeks following the murder Jose saw the dying man in his memory. In painful flashbacks, he watched him writhing in pain. Agonizing over the incident, Jose buried his guilt and shame with more drugs and more alcohol. His conscience was dulled. His mind was twisted. His heart was filled with bitterness.

Jose's years locked up in "La Casa Grande" hardened him to what seemed to be the point of no return. Some of his fellow prisoners tried to tell him that "Somebody" cared about him, but he was enraged by their words and refused to listen. Hate strangled every healthy emotion in Jose's heart like a deadly serpent.

But the old dream of being a good man flickered again in his heart when it was time for parole. Jose promised himself that he would turn his back on his addictions and his violent lifestyle. And for three weeks he did so. However, keeping promises—even to himself—wasn't one of Jose's habits, and before a month had passed he was back into his old ways again. He began dealing drugs in earnest, made himself a fortune, built a house, bought expensive cars, then lost everything when his drug network collapsed. Before he knew what had hit him, he was back on the streets of Oakland. And this time there was nobody to turn to— everybody in his old gang had turned against him.

Jose called his mother, who had moved to Northern California, asking if he could live with her.

She said, "*Amigo,* you will always have a room in my house, but you'll have to leave your drugs and alcohol behind. I don't want to live that way no more." In his desperation, Jose agreed to abide by her rules. He pretended to be clean for about a week, but soon he was stealing from her and living on booze and drugs both day and night.

One night, after an around-the-clock binge of alcohol and cocaine, his mother confronted him. "You're killing yourself," she cried, "and I don't want any part of it. Get out of my life!"

Jose's younger brother, who had always looked up to him, added his own words of rejection: "You have brought our family nothing but grief. I hate you, and I wish you were dead."

Jose was so hurt and angry that he grabbed his brother by the throat and began to strangle him. He watched the younger man's face change colors, and then, for some reason, stopped and threw him on the ground. While his brother gasped for air, Jose ran into his mother's bedroom. She was a Catholic, and he knew that she always prayed there.

To Jose, the concept of God had always seemed like a cruel joke—if He existed, why didn't He take better care of people? But that night, in his despair, Jose fell on his face before the unseen God. "If You are real," he sobbed, "take away my hunger for drugs. Take away my thirst for alcohol. Take away the rage in my heart. If You're real, give me a new life. I don't want to live like this anymore!"

Jose passed out, and he slept for hours. When he awoke he felt strangely rested and at peace. His mother had covered him with a blanket and had placed a pillow under his head. Beside the pillow was a note: "There is a Christian discipleship house where you can go live. Here's the address."

Jose, who had reached the end of his inner resources, located the house, a part of the Dream Center. The house director who interviewed him asked him how long it had been since he'd used cocaine. "Last night," Jose answered. "In fact, I've been high for three weeks."

"I believe you, but your hands aren't shaking, and you don't act like a man who's been using drugs for days on end. What else have you done?"

Only then did Jose remember his prayer. His voice broke as he told the man about his cry to God. "I asked God to help me, and I guess He did."

The house director nodded. "I want you to ask Jesus

Christ into your life right now. He's already begun the work in you. You need to invite Him in so He can finish it." The two men wept together as Jose prayed the sinner's prayer.

From that day, Jose was changed. His hatred and rage diminished hour by hour, and his addictions no longer haunted him. He began to study the Bible. Through his time in the Word and in prayer, Jose realized that God was calling him to reach out to other men who were caught in the lifestyle that he now describes as "the pit of hell."

Today Jose is not like his father. He isn't addicted to drugs and alcohol. He lives at the Dream Center, leading others out of drug addiction. Just as he promised his mother when he was nine years old, he has become—with God's help—a good man in what can sometimes be a bad world.

A Dream of Peace

BRIAN WAS A SICKLY CHILD, FRAIL AND THIN. HE WAS MOCKED and taunted for his skinniness and tormented by bullies. To make matters worse, his home life was a nightmare. As much as Brian longed for a peaceful, safe haven to call his own, his family situation was unbearable. His mother had divorced his father and was now married to a violent and abusive man. Brian's stepfather beat his wife frequently and occasionally even threatened her life with a gun.

Undersized and physically unfit, Brian was tortured by the powerlessness he felt. He longed to defend his mother, to protect her from her brutal spouse. But he was small and weak, and in his helplessness, he began to hate himself.

When he was old enough Brian joined the Marine Corps, hoping to become more of a man through the rigorous training. "I trained as hard as I could," he recalls, "just to get meaner and tougher."

In Saudi Arabia during the Gulf War, Brian killed for the

first time. Then he killed again. He killed in combat over and over—and he enjoyed it more every time. For the first time in his life, Brian felt a sense of power and control. But he had gained it through violence.

Once the war was over and he was discharged from the military, Brian had no outlet for his rage and no place to exercise his newfound love of brutality. Within ten months he was arrested for assault on three separate occasions.

He ended up on the streets of inner-city L.A., where he met a woman and fathered a child. Only then did the horror of his past catch up with him. As he looked at the beautiful, new life he had helped bring into the world, he was unable to cope with the flashbacks he was having of the beatings and killings he had so enjoyed. In his confusion and despair, Brian lost his way. He ended up on Skid Row, embittered and alone.

It was there that he encountered my son Matthew, who rather boldly announced to this violent man, "The Holy Spirit told me you need to get on this bus and come to church tonight."

Brian hesitated. He couldn't have been less interested in going to church. And he wasn't about to get on the bus.

"We're not leaving until you do," Matthew concluded.

Brian frowned menacingly. "Look, all I want is a shower and a bed," he growled.

"You'll get a shower and a bed. And a meal, too."

The first stop, however, was the Dream Center's church service. Brian later recalled, "I couldn't tell you what Matthew said or what the sermon was about. But I felt a peace that night that I had never felt in my entire life."

Months later Brian became the first graduate of the Dream Center's discipleship program. Today he is beginning a ministry of his own. He calls it MIA—Missing in America. Now that his own violence has been replaced by the peace he always dreamed about, he wants to share the gospel of Jesus Christ with others who are as lost as he was.

Dreams of Winning and Losing

IN HIGH SCHOOL MATTHEW WAS ONE OF THE BEST WRESTLERS in the state of Arizona. He won the state championship three years in a row, never losing one match in the process. And as his number-one fan, I never missed an opportunity to be on the sidelines. I yelled. I cheered. I coached. I was a wrestling enthusiast, so I pushed him toward greater skill, better technique, more success. I was a driver, so I drove him.

But I began to notice something. Although Matthew never lost, he was becoming increasingly nervous before every match. He trembled. He lost his appetite. He was afraid, even though he knew very well that he could and would win. It gradually dawned on me that Matthew was afraid to lose. Was it because he wondered how I'd react if he did?

Of course we had always dreamed that someday Matthew would be the national wrestling champion in his age and weight bracket. But I was beginning to cherish an even more important longing—I wanted to show my son how much I really loved him. And it seemed to me that the only way I could do that would be if he lost a match.

One of the problems wrestlers face is keeping their weight within rigid size categories. In order to fit into a lower-weight division where the competition was best suited for him, Matthew would virtually starve himself before the weigh-in. Sometimes he didn't even want to drink water; an extra ounce could make the difference in qualifying or not.

At one particular match pitting Matthew against a formidable opponent, he entered the competition in a weakened state. It wasn't long before he found himself losing the match—even though we all knew that Matthew could have easily outwrestled the young man if he had kept up his strength. But Matthew was devastated. He lifted himself unsteadily from the mat and began to cry.

When he cried, I cried, too. I picked him up and, along with his brother, Luke, carried him outside. He took him to a water fountain, poured water over his head, and held him close while he drank his fill.

"Matthew," I said, "we know you could whip that guy anytime you want to. The only reason you lost was because you were weak from not eating."

Matthew shook the water from his hair and studied my face. "Dad, I think I want to play basketball," he said.

"Son, you're a winner, no matter what sport you decide to play."

In his loss, my young son learned that we loved him because he was Matthew—not because he had defeated yet another opponent. He hadn't fulfilled his dream, but I had fulfilled mine. In losing, we had won.

Johnny Cash and My Davenport Dream

WHEN I FIRST BEGAN TO PASTOR IN DAVENPORT, IOWA, I WAS invited to preach at a revival in Nashville, Tennessee. It was a very small crusade and not many people came. But one of those who did show up was Johnny Cash's secretary. And after she heard me preach, she invited the country-singing star and his wife, June Carter Cash, to attend, too.

At that time Johnny Cash had recently turned his life around and recommitted himself to Christ. Several years later, when he was at the height of his success, he came to Davenport to put on a concert. I went to hear him, and afterward I found my way to his dressing room. I wasn't sure he'd remember me, but in case he did, I asked someone to give him a message. "Please tell Mr. Cash that Tommy Barnett is here and wants to see him," I said.

The messenger disappeared, and in the background I heard Johnny Cash's deep voice: "Tell the preacher to come in."

Sure enough, he did remember me. I decided to ask him for a favor. "I want to put on the world's largest Sunday school rally right here in Davenport, and I want you to come," I said. "I'm going to rent the local baseball stadium and invite everyone in town."

As a superstar, Johnny Cash was charging thousands of dollars for every appearance. But he agreed to come—and he wouldn't accept a penny from us. We rented the local baseball field and Johnny Cash arrived, bringing with him Carl Perkins, June Carter Cash, their two daughters, and Ma Carter.

Twenty-five thousand people gathered for that event. It was the largest crowd ever assembled in Davenport, and it made the front page of the newspapers—with stories reporting that six thousand people accepted Jesus Christ as their Lord and Savior.

Johnny Cash came back two years later for a similar rally, with similar results. I had a dream of reaching my part of the world for Jesus Christ—and the "Man in Black," Johnny Cash himself, helped me make that dream come true.

Dreams of Renewed Purity

OUR YOUTH GROUP IN DAVENPORT WAS FIRED UP FOR GOD, and they were troubled by the growing presence of X-rated magazines, books, and movies in our community. They decided to take a stand against pornography and asked me if I would object to their demonstrating in front of adult bookstores and theaters.

I called the city attorney to find out if such protests were legal. "The sidewalk belongs to everybody," the lawyer assured me. "It's a public area, and they can walk there anytime they want to."

The night of the demonstration arrived, and the kids enthusiastically hit the streets. A couple of hours after they were to have begun their "march," my phone rang. One of the boys excitedly reported, "Pastor Barnett, the police have ordered us off the streets!"

"This is America!" I encouraged him. "You have your rights. Go ahead and stay there."

An hour later, the phone rang again. "Pastor," a hesitant young voice said, "we're in jail. Can you come and get us out?"

I was furious. I stormed through the station door and startled the sheriff, who had his feet up on his desk. "Sheriff, " I roared, "you are in big trouble!"

Just then his phone rang. He answered, listened for a moment, and his face grew troubled. "Thirty more people have replaced these kids of yours," he informed me. "What am I going to do?"

"I'll tell you what you're going to do. If you don't let those kids out of here, there are going to be two thousand parents out there, and they aren't going to be any happier than I am."

The sheriff looked at me, his eyes pleading. "Look, Pastor, if you'll get those thirty people to leave the sidewalk, I'll let the kids out, and I'll try to do something about the adult bookstores and theaters," he said. "I'll try to stop this thing."

The sheriff was as good as his word. After that, pornographic magazines were either removed from store shelves or hidden under counters where they couldn't be seen except by request. Meanwhile, the local newspaper reported on the incident and announced that I would be preaching against pornography the following Sunday night. "Barnett Declares War on Pornography," the headline blared.

Since we had also taken a strong stand against the local massage parlors (which were serving as fronts for prostitution), our Sunday night service looked like a media circus. Not only were the local television stations and newspapers represented, but five young ladies who served as masseuses came to the church to stand up for their businesses and watch the "evil" Pastor Barnett in action.

That night, we were all in for a surprise. Our dream to renew a sense of purity in our community began to transform some of the very women who stood against us. Of the five who came to protest our stand against massage parlors, three repented of their sins and gave their lives to Jesus that very night. Since then an ordinance has been passed to keep massage parlors out of Davenport. It remains in effect to this very day.

Dreams and Real Protection

IN OUR VIOLENT WORLD, WE SOMETIMES DREAM OF FEELING completely safe. We try to ensure our security with a variety of alarms, guard dogs, cell phones, and fences. But our real protection doesn't necessarily come that way.

During the time our church was fighting against pornography and massage parlors in Davenport, Iowa, the massage parlor owners brought in a man from Chicago to get me off their backs. The Mafia owned the parlors, and the Chicago hit man was on the mob's payroll. His job was, at the very least, to terrorize us. And we had reason to believe that he might do far worse.

Aware of the danger, our family took every precaution we could. At night the police sent a helicopter to keep an eye on our house. Officers guarded our neighborhood. Our three children slept in the same room.

My wife, Marja, had only recently learned to drive and was not particularly skillful at the wheel. As she returned home one day from an outing, a man who had been parked along the roadside suddenly pulled out, tailgated her, and tried to drive her off the road. Realizing that she could not outmaneuver this man, Marja simply jumped out of the car and ran for the nearest farmhouse.

She had no idea who lived there, but she threw open the front door and ran inside. "Help me!" she cried out. "I'm being followed!"

The woman who lived in the house stared at Marja in disbelief. "How on earth did you get in? Who are you?"

"I'm Marja Barnett," she explained, "Pastor Barnett's wife. And I came in through the front door."

"You couldn't have," the woman insisted. "I just locked, chained, and bolted that door. There's no way you could have come in that way."

"But I did!" Marja insisted. "How else would I have gotten in?"

I don't know if it was divine intervention, or if the woman simply forgot to lock up. But I know this—when you are pursuing the dreams of God, God will take care of you. He's the greatest security we could ever have.

Vicarious Dreams

I LIVE ABOUT TWO HUNDRED MILES FROM THE GRAND CANYON. People come from all over the world to visit this great tourist attraction, which is an awe-inspiring example of God's creative artistry. But the truth is, I've never been to the Grand Canyon myself!

It's not that I don't want to see it—of course, I do. And I've made plans to travel there on more than one occasion. But it seems that every time the date of the scheduled trip arrives, somebody in the church gets sick and goes into the hospital or one of our young people needs counseling. Or there's a death or a wedding. The result is always the same: I have to cancel my plans. At this point, I don't know if I'll ever get to go.

And yet, in a way, I've already been there. Every year our church takes a busload of underprivileged kids—youngsters who live in the poorest areas of town, who often have been neglected, abused, or mistreated—to visit this world-famous national park. We fill our bus with boys and girls and head out to the Grand Canyon. I've never had the opportunity to go with them, but I always show up in the church parking lot to wave goodbye. I also make it a point, whenever I can, to be there when they return. They always come charging out of the bus, rushing to hug their parents and, with sparkling eyes, describe their amazing day.

One evening when I went out to meet the returning bus, a precious little black boy, his face absolutely wreathed in smiles, stepped out the door.

"Buddy," I asked him, "did you have a good time?"

"Good time?" he laughed out loud. "You wouldn't believe what a good time I had! And you wouldn't believe what I saw!"

"Try me."

"Preacher," he beamed, "I saw the biggest hole in the ground I've ever seen in my life!"

Of course that "hole in the ground" he described was one of the Seven Wonders of the World. As I returned to my office, I felt like jumping up and down. No, I've never been to the Grand Canyon, but I've seen the Grand Canyon through the eyes of that little boy.

I've had to set my own trip aside in order to meet the needs of my church people. But there are times when vicarious living is good enough, and for me this was one of those times. I was especially blessed knowing I had given up something so others could enjoy it. And at least one little boy had enjoyed that "big hole in the ground" more than I ever could have, even if I'd insisted on going there myself.

My Dream Come True

I SUPPOSE MOST MEN HAVE A DREAM CAR. FOR SOME, IT'S A hot-looking Mustang with a five-liter engine. For others, it's a Lexus with leather seats and a sunroof. For me, it was a Mercedes two-seat convertible. Of course, as a pastor, I have made a decision to be conservative in my lifestyle, so a car in that price range would not be appropriate. But there was no car in all the world that appealed to me more.

One day a tragedy struck our congregation. One night, late after work as a young woman and her husband were driving home, a drunk driver—a *wealthy* drunk driver—hit them broadside. The husband was killed instantly. Our church family gathered around the young widow and showered her with love and help, doing everything we could to look after her during such a heartbreaking time.

The young woman asked me to go to the funeral home with her. I helped her choose a casket and bought a huge bouquet of roses to place on top. I performed the funeral service and tried to offer comfort as the young man was buried amid prayers, tears, and an outpouring of compassion for his wife.

In the months that followed the young woman and her attorneys filed a lawsuit against the drunk driver. We rejoiced when we learned that it had resulted in an enormous settlement, which would make the widow financially secure for life. At least she would be well taken care of, even though no amount of money could compensate for the loss of her husband.

One afternoon, she appeared at my office. "Pastor," she said, "I want to show you something."

She took me outside, and I found myself staring at the most gorgeous Mercedes two-seat convertible I'd ever seen. "Congratulations!" I smiled at her. "It suits you well."

"No, you don't understand, Pastor. It's not for me. It's for you. The Lord wants me to give you this car as a token of my gratitude for all you did to help me."

Of course I knew immediately that I wouldn't—*couldn't!*—accept the car, but the woman's generosity was very touching. "Thank you so much," I told her. "I can't accept the car, but I really appreciate your wanting to give it to me."

"Pastor, please! " she insisted. "The Lord has impressed on me that you should have this car."

I was quite sure that the Lord was impressing something very different on me, but instead of arguing, I suggested, "Let's pray about this for a week, and we'll see what He does."

I already knew the answer, but I didn't want to hurt the woman. A week later the young widow came back, determined as ever. "I *know* the Lord wants me to give you this car."

I shook my head. "I'll tell you what I think the Lord wants. I think He wants you to be *willing* to give me the car. And if that's not right, then I'm the one who's wrong, not you."

She drove away, disappointed, but satisfied. I went to my office and prayed, feeling an unexpected sense of joy in my heart. I realized that I was able to rejoice in the fact that God had given me the desire of my heart. I *could* have had the car of my dreams. And that was all I needed to know.

My son Luke, however, interpreted the situation somewhat differently. "Sure, the Lord told her to give the car to somebody named Barnett," he laughed good-naturedly. "She just got the first name wrong. She was supposed to give it to *Luke* Barnett!"

A Dream Journey

WHEN I WAS ABOUT TO TURN SIXTY, I TOLD MY CHURCH, "I'M going to do something unusual to celebrate the goodness of God in my life for the past sixty years." But what could I do? Finally I decided. When I was a young man, I'd had a dream of running across America. Now was the time! I would take my two-week vacation to walk from Phoenix to Los Angeles—a four-hundred-mile trek. I would use the walk to raise funds, and whatever money came in would be used to refurbish the Dream Center. People were enthusiastic and sponsored my "Dream Journey" generously.

The trek started out well—I walked thirty-five miles the first day. The next day I figured I could do forty. But by noon, blisters were puffing up all over my feet and the joints of my hips were throbbing. Limping along a deserted dirt road, I hadn't seen a car for hours except for the one that was following me on the trip. Suddenly a pickup truck roared to a near stop alongside me. A handsome young

Native American man who looked about thirty years old rolled down his window. "Are you okay?"

"I'm fine," I assured him.

"Where are you going?"

"I'm walking to Los Angeles."

"L.A.? You've got to be kidding. Why are you walking to L.A.?"

I told him that I was a pastor, that my church had bought the old Queen of the Angels Hospital there, and that we were refurbishing it to create a place called the Dream Center.

"Tell me about the Dream Center," he said.

"Well, it will be a place where people can live and get help with their problems," I explained. "We'll take in drug addicts, alcoholics, runaway kids, and prostitutes—anybody who needs our help."

The man's eyes brimmed with tears. "That's where I need to go. I have a drug problem and a drinking problem."

I talked to him for quite a while, and once I'd assured him that he could visit the Dream Center, I asked him if there was a shortcut across the area of desert we were crossing. "Yes, there is," he nodded. "There's a shortcut through the reservation."

He got in the car that was following me to personally guide us and make sure we didn't get lost. As I walked in front of the car, Gary, my friend who was driving, led the young man to Jesus Christ.

"I want to get baptized," he said after he and Gary prayed together.

"Well, that's a good idea, but there's no water in the desert," Gary reminded him.

"But I want to be baptized."

Suddenly Gary remembered the bottled water we were carrying in the trunk of the car. Now we aren't Methodists, who baptize by pouring, but as we sometimes say, "The ox was in the ditch." Gary stopped, opened a bottle of Evian water, and poured it over the new believer's head.

The man had some pending legal problems, and Gary went with him to court where his sentence was reduced. He's now out of prison. Soon he will be fully immersed in baptism at our church. He plans to live at the Dream Center in Los Angeles. And he gave me a wonderful confirmation: Through him, my "Dream Journey" came to represent every aspect of the work we are trying to do in Los Angeles.

Dreams and Disappointments

SOMETIMES WE DREAM OF SHINING THE LIGHT OF GOD'S GLORY into the darkness of the secular world. And sometimes those dreams end in what looks like defeat. Maybe we underestimate the power of the enemy. Or maybe we overestimate the importance of the world's approval. This has been made clear to me more than once, but one particular incident was especially disappointing.

Some of the leaders in my denomination asked me to cooperate with the journalists who were writing an article about the Assemblies of God for the *Wall Street Journal*. Because recent scandals had rocked the world with stories about fallen Christian leaders, we all hoped that a positive piece would help defuse the public's growing cynicism about Christian ministry. I was less than enthusiastic, however, simply because I had been burned before by a prejudiced press and wasn't excited about having to endure a repeat performance.

Nevertheless, I agreed, and sat down with a pleasant reporter named Robert Johnson. He assured me that his intentions were nothing but honorable and that he was very open-minded. I spent hours with the man. I personally took him around our facilities and gave him a close-up look at our many community-outreach programs. I was delighted when he attended a Sunday morning service and came forward in response to my altar call for salvation. And as he left town, he assured me that he would write a positive article. I believed him.

When the story ran, however, under the headline "Heavenly Gifts" were subheads: "Preaching a Gospel of Acquisitiveness, a Showy Sect Prospers," and "After TV-Minister Scandals, Assemblies of God Emerge Bigger, Richer Than Ever." One subhead simply read, "Praying for a Honda Accord." The text of the article was even worse than the headlines.

Letters and phone calls inundated our church and our denominational headquarters. People were infuriated. Some of them wanted to sue the *Wall Street Journal*. Others wanted to know if we were being faithful stewards of their donations. As for me, I felt personally betrayed, lied to, and shamefully treated. I wrote a letter to the journalist, taking responsibility for anything I might have said or done to mislead him in his view of our ministry. I humbled myself and left the results with the Lord. But still I struggled.

As is often the case, meditating upon the work and words of Jesus helped me resolve my bitter disappointment. Describing the Crucifixion, the Gospel of Matthew tells us, "And when they came to a place called Golgotha (which means the place of a skull), they offered him wine to drink, mingled with gall; but when he tasted it, he would not drink it" (Matt. 27:33–34, RSV).

Gall is a poisonous herb. When Jesus tasted the gall in the wine, He spit it out. He would have nothing to do with it.

The message was clear and comforting. Like gall, bitterness is poisonous, too. And when dreams turn to bitter disappointments, we ought to follow Jesus' example and spit out the bitterness—otherwise it will poison our lives for a very long time.

Dreams and a New Beginning

BILL WILSON'S FAMILY FELL APART WHEN HE WAS BARELY A teenager. His parents moved to Florida, where his father left his mother. She went to work as a bartender, and before long she was bringing home an assortment of male friends from the tavern who shared her addiction to alcohol. Eventually one of them moved into the house, and he became violently abusive of her. At about the same time, Bill learned that his father was dead.

Bill drifted further and further away from home, sometimes not eating for days at a time. For a while he hoped that somehow his life would take a turn for the better, but that dream didn't last long. Instead he wandered the streets of Florida, bumming meals and becoming more cynical and hopeless with every passing day. Bill was hungry, skinny, struggling with rickets and a facial disfigurement. He was fairly sure that dreams weren't for lost kids like him.

One day, after watching from a distance as a man in Bill's

neighborhood tuned a racecar, Bill finally summoned the courage to walk over and watch close up. The racecar driver introduced himself to the ragged-looking adolescent and initiated a life-changing friendship. Bill liked the man and felt he was sincerely a good person. "At least he acted like he cared," Bill says.

Back home, Bill's life with his mother was going from bad to worse. "I was fourteen years old then. My mother and I were walking down the street on the block where we lived in Pinellas Park, Florida—just north of St. Petersburg. It was near the Welcome Inn on Park Boulevard, where she worked as a barmaid.

"We stopped and sat down on a concrete culvert that was built over a little drainage ditch. She was very quiet that day. After a few minutes she stood up and said, 'I can't do this anymore. You wait here.' *What was she talking about?* I wondered. *What is it she can't do anymore?*

"I did exactly what my mom said. I sat there waiting for her to return. The sun went down, and she still wasn't back.

"The next day I sat on that same culvert, alone with my thoughts. I thought about the nights that my mom didn't come home. Was that happening again? Surely she'd be back soon.

"For three days I sat in the Florida sun on that hot, concrete culvert. I didn't know where to turn. My sister had married and moved to New Jersey. Dad was gone. If I had known how to pray, I would have done it, but religion had no place in our home.

"All I could do was try to be brave and choke back the tears that would fill up my eyes.

"Mom never came back."

After three days, Dave Rudenis, the man with the racecars, noticed Bill sitting there . . . alone. Dave stopped his car and walked over to Bill, and they began to talk. Dave was also a deacon at a local church in St. Petersburg, Florida.

"How would you like to go to youth camp?" Dave asked Bill.

"What's that?" Bill responded.

"Oh, you'd love it. Lots of kids your age will be there. They have softball, swimming, and great services." Dave Rudenis paid the week's tuition for Bill—$17.50—and put him in the pastor's station wagon with some other teens.

The food filled his empty stomach, but it was somewhat lacking in flavor. The rules were confining to a boy who lived unsupervised on the streets. But one night, Bill Wilson heard the preacher say, "If you need Jesus, come to the front."

Looking back, Bill says, "I wasn't crying, I wasn't emotional at all, but I knew I needed something. And this was it. I got up, walked down to the front, and knelt there all by myself. That's when I accepted Christ."

Meanwhile, a new pastor arrived at the local church where Bill was now attending. He allowed Bill to live in the church evangelists' quarters, and he also encouraged him to go to Bible college. He gave Bill, who was now working in a garage, the responsibility for the church's dilapidated bus, which had been used to pick up kids for Vacation Bible School. "If you can't come up with a reason for keeping that bus, we'll have to sell it," the pastor cautioned him.

Bill Wilson wasn't so sure that the church should get rid of the bus. Read the next story, and you'll find out what happened. As Bill puts it, "The rest is all history now."

An Unlikely Dreamer

MY FIRST ENCOUNTER WITH AN UNLIKELY DREAMER NAMED Bill Wilson took place at what I now call "the worst revival I ever had." The pastor of the St. Petersburg church was an outstanding evangelist himself. "I keep everybody saved," he told me when I arrived. "I have altar calls after every sermon. You might want to address the saints."

I listened politely, but I quickly dismissed his advice. After all, I was an evangelist, and evangelists are supposed to preach to the unsaved, aren't they? That's exactly what I did—and the results were exactly what he predicted. Few people were saved, and I felt downcast.

But one day a young man at the church asked if he could talk to me. He was skinny with long hair. I guess I'd have to say he wasn't the most attractive guy in town. But Bill had heard about my dad, who was well-known in some circles as the founder of an enormous bus ministry. That's why he wanted to talk to me.

"We've got one old bus here," he explained, "and I'm the driver, but they're thinking of getting rid of it. What am I supposed to do to turn this one little bus into a ministry?"

I studied the earnest young man's face. "I'll tell you what you have to do," I said. "You have to think of the people who ride your bus as your congregation. And you have to take care of those people like you'd take care of your own little church. Why don't you try that?"

"I think I will," he nodded.

It wasn't long before his new ministry began to thrive. The St. Petersburg church bought more buses, and Bill Wilson made sure that every one of them had a godly bus pastor.

Sometime later, a tragic death took place, and Bill lost his pastor. He called me in Davenport and said, "I want to come and help you. How would you feel about me becoming your bus pastor?"

Bill Wilson came to Iowa, and it wasn't long before he had forty-seven buses operating in Davenport, reaching thousands of people.

Eventually God called me to Phoenix, and when I left for Phoenix, Bill felt led to go to New York City. He began to run buses in the worst part of Brooklyn. Today, after years of faith and persistence, his ministry reaches over twenty thousand people in New York City. Metro Ministries is the largest Sunday school in America, thanks to God and Bill Wilson's dream of being the best church bus driver he could be. Right now, Metro Ministries' program for reaching people in the inner city is succeeding in hundreds of cities around the world. As for Bill, he is also a famous evangelist and seminar speaker.

Dreams and Handshakes

DECADES AGO I HEARD AN INTERESTING STORY ABOUT President John F. Kennedy. The day he and his wife, Jacqueline, arrived in Dallas—the day of his assassination— he reminded her that he wasn't a popular man in that part of the country. "We've got a lot of enemies here in Dallas," he told her, "so walk slowly through the crowd. Look everybody in the eye. And shake every hand."

Not long ago, during the Christmas season, I walked outside the church at about 5:00 P.M. on a Sunday afternoon. I had preached for the morning service and for the 3:00 P.M. Christmas pageant, and I would soon be back to preach for the pageant at 7:00 P.M. In fact, people were already lining up for it.

I was exhausted, and as I quickly headed toward my office, I noticed a couple standing by a church doorway. I don't believe in passing anyone without a greeting, so I walked over and said, "Hello, folks. I'm pleased to meet you."

After some small talk, the man said, "You know, we came all the way from North Carolina to see this pageant."

"North Carolina? I can't believe you came all that way! Thank you so much for coming!"

The man nodded affably, and then he asked, "So how's your work in L.A. doing? I know you need some money to finish."

"Oh, well, it's good," I replied. "The money's going to come."

The man was persistent. "You now, we'd be very interested in helping you with that work. Do you have time to talk to us for a few minutes? We didn't expect to run into you, but since you stopped . . ."

We went to my office, and that generous man began to share his heart. Before many minutes had passed, he said the most amazing thing: "My wife and I would like to give you one hundred thousand dollars to help you buy your building in Los Angeles." He wrote out a check right then and there. A few months later, he sent another check for forty thousand dollars. Their generosity has been a wonderful blessing—and above and beyond that, they have also become dear friends.

John Kennedy was right—it always pays to walk slowly through the crowd. It pays to take the time to talk to every person. To look everyone in the eye. To shake one hand at a time. Because if you are willing to spend extra time, energy, and love, you may just find yourself shaking hands, for the first time, with a lifelong friend.

A Dream of a Good Investment

ONE PART OF MY DAY IS VERY PRECIOUS TO ME, AND I GUARD it jealously. I really enjoy driving out in the morning, buying a cup of coffee and a newspaper, and sitting alone in my car while I read the paper. It's a time of complete privacy, a peaceful break in my busy life, and I don't like to have it interrupted.

One morning I was parked in front of a convenience store with my head in the newspaper when a car pulled up next to me and blasted its horn. Startled by the sudden noise, I glanced up. The driver quickly rolled down his window. He looked a little ragged but not especially desperate.

"I don't want to bother you," he explained, "but I need to replace this tire, and I'm short twenty dollars." He motioned toward a rear tire that looked as if it needed some air. "There's a tire store right over there," he said, pointing to a mall across the road, "and if you'll loan me twenty dollars, I'll pay you back. I'll pay you back this week. Just write your name and address on a piece of paper, and I'll mail you the money."

I wasn't especially pleased with having my few moments of quiet interrupted, and I was even less pleased with the man's appeal for money. I was pretty sure that this was one of the best scams I'd heard yet. Nevertheless, something inside me said, "Do it!"

I reached for my wallet and pulled out a twenty-dollar bill. "Look," I told him, "I'm going to give this to you. I'm a minister—I'm the pastor of that church on the side of the mountain over there. And I want you to understand something. This money was given to me. It's God's money. It needs to go for that tire and nothing else. And the way to pay me back is to come to church this Sunday. Don't bother to send me any money. Just come up to me after the service and say hello. That's all you have to do."

The man eagerly took the money, vowing, "I'll be there. I promise!"

"Just come up and let me know, " I told him again.

The next Sunday I looked for the man, but he was nowhere to be seen. We have a huge congregation, and I knew that he could easily be there without my seeing him. But he didn't come up and find me that Sunday—or any of the Sundays that followed.

I wrote off the twenty dollars and forgot all about it.

A year later, at the end of an altar call, a man came up to shake my hand. "Do you recognize me?" he asked.

"You look familiar, but . . ."

"I'm the guy you gave twenty dollars to a year ago. Don't you remember? You gave me the money for a tire. Well, today I came to your church, and just now I prayed and accepted Jesus. So the debt is paid, right?"

I embraced him and said, "Brother, that's not all that's paid. The debt for your sins was paid on Calvary. And that's the most important debt of all."

A Daydream

SOME YEARS AGO I PREACHED AT A REVIVAL IN SOUTH BEND, Indiana. My schedule was grueling, and to make matters worse, I was already tired when I arrived. After preparing my messages, preaching for hours, and talking to people, I was only averaging two or three hours of sleep every night.

The church had scheduled a television broadcast for me, and they informed me that I would have to be up by 5:00 A.M. that morning to make it to the studio on time. At first I agreed. But in my deep exhaustion, I began to daydream about skipping the show and sleeping in. Just one morning's worth of extra sleep, and I knew I'd feel so much better! The more I thought about it, the better it sounded.

At the service that night I located the woman who had arranged the TV appearance and called her aside. "I am so grateful for all you're doing to bless my ministry, but I'm so tired I can hardly see straight," I confided. "I'm too tired to be on TV tomorrow morning. Could I skip the program?"

The woman was very gracious and promised to call the station early the next morning to cancel the arrangements. At first I was relieved, but as the evening passed I felt increasingly uncomfortable with my decision.

I collapsed in bed that night, but as tired as I was, I couldn't sleep. Something inside me said, "You'd better be on that program."

Halfheartedly I crawled out of bed, located the woman's phone number, and dialed it. "I'm sorry to call so late," I explained, "but I've changed my mind. I'll be at the studio tomorrow as we originally planned."

I showed up and completed the TV appearance as promised, but I was uninspired. It seemed pretty obvious to me that I was just too worn out to make much of an impression on anybody. I did, however, remember to mention a specific need that our ministry was facing. We needed four million dollars to buy the Dream Center. And we only had one and one-half years to come up with the remaining money—nearly three million dollars. When I left South Bend later that day, I was physically drained. I second-guessed my decision to keep the scheduled appearance. *It wasn't really worth it,* I thought. *I was too tired to do a good job. I should have stayed in bed.*

A few weeks later I was busy with a thousand other things. I hadn't thought about South Bend for several days. My assistant brought in the mail, and when I opened one particular envelope, I caught my breath in astonishment. Inside was a check for thirty-nine thousand dollars! A letter explained that the donor had watched the program that had been broadcast from South Bend, Indiana. He had noticed that I seemed weary. He had been moved by my words—he wanted to have a part in helping meet our ministry's needs!

Recaptured Dreams

THERE IS A WOMAN IN OUR PHOENIX CONGREGATION WHO had it all—money, diamonds, furs, luxurious holidays abroad. Carol Blust Swegle had won beauty contests and had even worked as a fashion model. Her storybook life was crowned with the best of everything when she married a wealthy professional and gave birth to two beautiful daughters. All her dreams seemed to have come true.

But behind all the beauty, glamour, and wealth, Carol wasn't as happy as she seemed. Once her little girls started school, the emptiness inside her grew wider and deeper and more dangerous. She tried to fill her life with activity, with charity work, with homemaking, but to no avail. When all else failed, Carol began to drink.

A concerned family doctor prescribed antidepressants and tranquilizers and referred her to a psychiatrist. Carol tried the pills, then tried mixing them with the alcohol, which left her more despondent than ever. Nothing seemed to lift her out of the deep, dark void that engulfed her soul.

Two days before her second appointment with her psychiatrist, Carol became so disoriented that she tried to commit suicide. She knew nothing about guns, but she tried to shoot herself with one anyway. The bullet pierced her neck and severed her spinal cord. In a heartbeat, Carol was a quadriplegic.

Countless surgeries and hospital stays followed. Since she could not take care of herself, she ended up in a local nursing home—the youngest resident there at only thirty-two years old. A janitor at the home was troubled by the sight of this beautiful young woman who was so crippled and so sad. He invited her to a revival meeting at his church.

Carol agreed to go. She went once with the janitor, and then she went again. Night after night, she returned to the revival. She listened carefully to the message that Jesus loved her, that He died for her, that He could forgive her past.

Was Jesus really the answer?

With growing hope, Carol wheeled herself to the front of the church with the help of her special mouth-operated wheelchair and prayed, "Lord, if You will take me just as I am, I'll serve You for the rest of my life."

Instantly Carol was immersed in joy. Her emptiness and anger were washed away in the tide of God's unconditional love and forgiveness. Even her desire for alcohol was gone. Many friends had abandoned her. Her husband had rejected her. Her body was broken and useless. But Jesus loved her. He was always there. And He still had a plan for her life.

Eleven years later a wonderful man came into Carol's life at a Christian retreat center in North Carolina. She admired him as he eloquently prayed a blessing on the food. He admired her beautiful, radiant face. They were married, and today they are serving God side by side. It may sound unlikely, but if you ask her, she will assure you that it's true: Carol Swegle's life is more joyful and rewarding now than it ever was before.

The $100,000 Dream

About to fly out of Phoenix to speak at a conference in Dallas, I ducked into a pay-phone booth to call my assistant with last minute instructions about some upcoming sermons. As I mentioned the title of one of the sermons, "What to Do if You Miss the Rapture," I was vaguely aware that a black man in the phone booth next to me was suddenly captivated by what I was saying. I finished my call and was about to head back to the gate when he caught up with me and began to walk alongside.

"Excuse me for listening to your conversation," he began, "but I heard you speaking about the Rapture. Are you a minister?"

"Yes, I'm a pastor," I answered.

"Where?"

"My church is in Phoenix."

"Tell me about your church. I'd like to know more about it," he said.

Something about his curiosity intrigued me. Then he told me he was a pastor, too.

"Look," I told him, "we have a pastors' school every year, and I'd like for you to be at the next one." I gave him all the necessary information, and he agreed to attend.

That year's conference began right on schedule, and as usual, over seven thousand pastors and workers were touched and blessed night after night. One night a black man walked up to the platform during the offering. I immediately recognized him as my airport acquaintance. To my amazement, he began to speak into a microphone.

"I've been so touched by this conference," he told the huge crowd. "I'm never going to be the same, and I'll bet you aren't, either. And I think we should give a generous offering to Tommy Barnett's church tonight—a special offering to bless him for what he's doing for us. I feel that they have a special need right now." He pulled a checkbook out of his pocket. "I'm going to give one thousand dollars," he announced. "What are you going to give?"

That grateful, generous pastor had a dream of blessing our church in a special way. And he had no way of knowing that we had, just days before, received an unexpected bill in the amount of one hundred thousand dollars for bus insurance. Thanks to him, over one hundred thousand dollars was received in that one offering! He blessed me more than I could have possibly blessed him.

God's Dream Fulfilled

As a young boy, I didn't have to look far for a role model. My dad was my hero. He could hit a ball farther than anybody else. He could accomplish whatever he set his mind and hand to more completely than anybody else. And he could encourage me like nobody else on earth. Dad had grown up with wonderful parents who could be somewhat negative at times, but instead of being embittered, he had long since decided to become a positive man. And in my eyes, he was the most positive influence ever to touch my life.

When I went to Dad's funeral, I was intensely involved in the various formalities from early morning until late at night. In years past, Dad had run for mayor. He had been on the school board for seventeen years. He was one of most beloved men in Kansas City, pastoring what was at that time the largest church in our denomination. People showed up from far and wide, and the outpouring of affection and appreciation was overwhelming. After the funeral service was over, we followed the hearse to the cemetery. As the hearse rolled down the town's main street, businessmen who loved my dad came out of their places of business to watch. Man after man removed his hat and placed his hand over his heart.

After a long, emotional day, I headed home, leaving my wife, Marja, to stay with my mother for the weekend. I boarded the plane back to Phoenix, and as that big jet lifted off the runway, I realized that I had never felt so alone in all my life. Hot tears ran down my cheeks. A thousand questions spun around in my mind: *Whom will I call every Sunday after I preach? Whom will I talk to when I'm happy? Who will rejoice with me? When I'm sad, who will weep with me?*

My dad had taught me how to build a church from the ground up. But he had taught by example as much as by words. As I've often said, some things are taught, while some things are caught—and I had caught a heavenly vision from my father. Now who would help me build my church?

I sat weeping in that aircraft, overwhelmed by loneliness. But as the plane droned on through the night, I heard a still, small voice: "If you'd just let Me, I'd like to comfort you. I'd like to rejoice with you. I'd like to help you build your church."

I knew immediately that I was no longer alone.

You see, the day my dad died, I saw the Lord for the very first time. Always before, my relationship had been second-hand; I had known the Lord through Dad. But now I had a firsthand revelation. From that day on, everything meant more. Prayer meant more. Instead of being a thirty-minute obligation, it was transformed into the desire of my heart, and my prayertime often extended from minutes into hours. At last my faith wasn't inherited; it was inherent.

Maybe God had always dreamed that someday He and I would walk together—just the two of us. The day my dad died, I saw the Lord waiting to walk with me. And He's been there, walking and talking with me, every day, ever since.

A Dad and a Dream

ONE OF THE MOST PRECIOUS MEMORIES I HAVE OF MY DAD IS the phone call he and I shared every Sunday evening after a dizzy day of preaching and services. I would call him or he would call me, and we would talk over the experiences we'd had that day ministering to our congregations and seeing men, women, and children saved.

One Sunday night I went to my office weary and worn. I had preached three times that day, and it had taken everything out of me. I opened the office door and was startled to see my son Matthew, who was about thirteen years old.

"I didn't expect to find you here," I told him, wondering why he hadn't already gone home.

"Dad," he explained, "I got to thinking about all the people who love you. Some of them would pay to have an opportunity to hear you preach. And I realized that I'm really privileged to live with you, to listen to you, and to have you as a father. I know that there are probably many people who would *pay* for an opportunity to ride home with you in the car. I just wanted to be the one who got to ride with you tonight."

I wiped my tears from my eyes and together we got into the car and headed home. Matthew and I talked the whole way, and it was a precious time.

My children have all moved away from home now, and even though I'm proud of the great things they're doing with their lives, at times I wish they were still around. But now we have car phones. And on Sunday nights I get calls from Matthew and Luke, who are both ministering in churches of their own. Either I call them or they call me, and we talk about our day of ministry, just as Dad and I used to do. For me, those are dream phone calls—because I have the best kids a father could ever dream of.

Dream Friends

MARIA WAS ONE OF THE LOCAL WOMEN WHO BENEFITED from our Dream Center's "Adopt-a-Block" program. Every Saturday our teams visit their designated neighborhood blocks, doing whatever needs to be done to lend a helping hand, to provide much needed food and clothing, and most of all, to share the love of Jesus Christ. Sometimes they mow lawns, paint apartment buildings, fix appliances, or help with clean-up projects. But building relationships— and inviting the neighbors to church—is Adopt-a-Block's first priority.

Maria was a very quiet person. Although the Dream Center team visited her every week, she rarely said much about herself. She was always polite, but it wasn't often that anyone saw her smile, and even then her eyes never seemed to lose their sadness. The team learned that she was a single mother from Central America, and it was evident that she lived in poverty with her two children. That's all they knew about Maria.

After several months Maria finally found the courage to attend a church service. She was welcomed with open arms. On her very first visit, she went forward and received Jesus Christ as her Savior. Everyone who knew her was ecstatic. From that time on, visits with her were warmer and less awkward, but still she never lost her shyness and reserve.

One Saturday, when the team knocked at Maria's door, nobody answered. They persisted for several minutes, until finally a neighbor appeared. The woman walked over with an uncertain expression on her face. "Haven't you heard?" she said. "Maria was killed yesterday."

"Killed? What do you mean?" The Adopt-a-Block team looked at each other in horror.

The neighbor nodded mutely but seemed reluctant to tell them more. Just then another more talkative neighbor arrived and recounted the terrible story. Maria's boyfriend had become angry with her and had pushed her in front of a moving car. She died instantly.

Maria's mother came from New York to Los Angeles for the funeral, and the Dream Center provided the facilities, food, and volunteer help necessary to make the occasion as pleasant as possible. The distraught mother wept inconsolably during the service. Afterward she spoke to my son Matthew.

"Maria didn't talk to you much—I know that, because she didn't talk much to anybody," she said. "But she wrote me a letter about you. She said you were the only friends she had in Los Angeles. Every week she looked forward to you coming to her door. She always dreamed that she would find friends here, and because of you, she did. Thank you for being there for my daughter."

As tragic as her death was, we all agreed that Maria had found an even better friendship than anyone at the Dream Center could possibly provide. She had found Jesus, and now she was with Him for all eternity.

Shattered Dreams

THE DREAM CENTER BUS GOES OUT EVERY WEEK, PICKS UP AS many street people as it can hold, and takes them to church. Sometimes hundreds of homeless people are brought in. They attend a worship service, then receive a good meal afterward.

For a while, one man often came on the bus. He was depressed and quiet, with a sinister expression on his face. Of course, there are many scary-looking people on the streets of Los Angeles but this man's expression seemed unusually evil.

After one service the man approached my son Matthew and pulled him aside. Everyone had left the building by then, and the two men stood alone. "I can't live anymore," he informed Matthew. "I'm dying of AIDS. But I know how you can get the news media to come to this church and cover the story of my death."

"How's that?" Matthew asked, feeling more uncomfortable with every word.

"I'm going to draw attention to myself by killing you and then killing myself."

The man reached into his pocket and pulled out a gun.

Matthew remained calm and looked the man directly in the eyes. "You can kill me, but I'll go to heaven, so you can't scare me with that," he said. "My concern is about you. What will happen to you when you kill yourself? Where will you go?"

The man brusquely pushed Matthew aside, threatened to come back and kill him in the month of March, and hurried off.

Unfortunately, when March arrived, he reappeared—just as he said he would. Every week he sat somewhere in the congregation, laughing at Matthew. He tried to stare him down, to intimidate him. After each service he would say, "Which week is it going to be?" Then he'd slip out the door hurriedly before Matthew could respond.

Naturally, there was a great deal of prayer going on about this matter. And after two or three weeks of uncertainty, at the end of one service, the troubled man asked to speak to Matthew.

This is it, Matthew thought, preparing himself for the worst. The strange-looking derelict pulled my son over to the side of the room, looked at him intently, and said, "Something happened to me this week. I was just walking down the road one day and conviction came over me. I realized what I was about to do. You see, I don't hate you, but I hate myself. And every time I see you, I see what I could have been if I hadn't wasted my life and shattered my dreams."

All at once the wretched man began to weep, and Matthew was able to lead him to Jesus Christ. With supernatural love, Matthew continued to hold him in his arms while he wept throughout the afternoon. In the weeks that followed, he sometimes came back to the Dream Center.

Matthew even had lunch one afternoon with his former stalker. Eventually the church paid the man's way back to his home in San Francisco, where he could be treated for his AIDS. By now he is probably with the Lord—living a new, unshattered life in his heavenly home.

Macho Dreams

AFTER PREACHING AT A REVIVAL IN BELL GARDENS, CALIFORNIA, which is now part of Los Angeles, I drove through the city streets to catch a plane back to Davenport, Iowa. In those days, there was no freeway connection to Los Angeles International Airport. The only way to the airport went through Watts, a notoriously rough neighborhood.

As I drove along that day, a car suddenly speeded around me and screeched to a halt in front of my vehicle. A guy jumped out, came toward me with a knife, and said, "Get out!"

I didn't respond. I simply backed up, passed him, and drove away. In my rear view mirror I saw him jump into his car and continue driving. At the next stoplight he pulled up next to me. His windows were down; my driver's window was rolled down a little way, too. The man was staring straight ahead, an angry expression fixed on his face, and I could see that he was breathing heavily.

I was furious and could not keep my feelings to myself. The "macho man" in me took over, and I yelled through the window, "You're really a big man with that knife, aren't you? How big are you without it?"

Without a word, the man pulled out a big gun. He didn't speak. He simply raised it up and shot. He couldn't have missed me by more than a couple of inches. The bullet went through my partially rolled-down window and shattered the back glass.

Angrier than ever, I took off after him and followed him until he leaped out of the car and ran into a house. A few minutes later, he left in the car again. By then I had telephoned the police and told them I wanted to prosecute.

My foolish, macho words almost cost me my life. At the time I only had two children. If that bullet had been more accurate, I would have never had Matthew. I would have never ministered in Phoenix. And there would have been no Los Angeles Dream Center. I would have had no impact on our nation or the world.

Today, I compare my own thoughtless, youthful outburst with the more mature behavior of my son Matthew, who now ministers in the inner city of Los Angeles. When he was threatened with a gun, Matthew was not concerned about posturing or showing off. Matthew had a soft, godly answer, and it turned away his assailant's wrath.

If Matthew had been in my place at that intersection, I know he would have handled the situation differently. If Matthew had been there instead of me, there would have been no harsh words and no shooting. In fact, knowing my son, he probably would have managed to lead that troubled young man to Christ. One macho moment almost halted the destiny of many lives.

One Man's Disappointment, Another Man's Dream

THE BIBLE CAUTIONS US ABOUT A COUPLE OF VERY IMPORTANT matters. For one thing, it warns us not to despise small things (Zech. 4:10). It also warns us not to despise a man's youth (1 Tim. 4:12).

When I was a young man, I wanted a pastorate very badly. I was a successful evangelist, but in those days the perception seemed to prevail that evangelists did not make good pastors. It was my dream to have a church of my own, so I wrote to churches over the country to put my name out as a candidate for a pastoral position. I really didn't care too much where I ended up. I put my name out to big churches; none of them wrote back. I put my name out to medium-sized churches; none of them wrote back. I put my name out to small churches; none of them wrote back either.

God eventually opened a door for me to start pastoring. Years later I met a man who began to shower me with gratitude. "I want to thank you *so much*," he gushed.

"Whatever for?" I asked, not having any idea who he was or what I had done to deserve his profuse praise.

"I'm so grateful to you, Pastor Barnett. You see, it was because of you that I was chosen to pastor my church in Independence, Missouri. And it's such a wonderful church!"

I was still bewildered. "I apologize, but I really don't remember recommending you," I explained, feeling a little embarrassed.

"Let me tell you what happened," he grinned. "For several years I went to try out for different pastorates, and every year somebody turned me down. One year when the search committee in Independence gathered to make a final decision, one of the elders bluntly rejected me. 'I think the man is too young,' he said of me.

"Another agreed. 'I think we need more experience. We need an older man.'

"But one elderly gentleman shook his head in disagreement. 'Let me remind you,' he admonished them, 'that forty years ago a young man named Tommy Barnett wrote to us because he wanted to come and pastor this church. We thought he was too young and inexperienced, and we turned him away. Today he pastors Phoenix First Assembly of God, which is one of the largest churches in the country. I don't think we should turn this man away. He's just what we need.'"

The young pastor gave me a huge grin. "You see, because they turned you down and you did so well afterward, today I'm pastoring the church of my dreams!"

A Dream of Restored Identity

ALEX DIDN'T LIKE HIMSELF. HE GREW UP IN A HISPANIC HOME where the males practiced extreme macho behavior. His father was a laborer, a hard man who drank heavily, fought fiercely, and physically abused his wife. Alex watched his father, his uncles, and his older brothers as they lived out the tough, mean behavior that they identified as "manly." And the more he watched, the more confused he was by his own sensitivity.

His confusion increased greatly when, as an adolescent, the male members of his family began to mock him for the tears he often shed and for the gentle emotions he found so difficult to hide. "You're a fag," they told him. "You're a queer. You don't belong in this family!"

Fearing that they were right, Alex joined the United States Navy and became what he now describes as a "hell-raiser"—a drunken, womanizing sailor. He lived that way for four years, becoming an award-winning seaman in the process and gaining the confidence of superior officers and shipmates alike. He served in Kuwait, Bosnia, and Somalia. Off duty, he drank, swore, smoked, and chased women. But in the privacy of his own heart, Alex could not have been more miserable. He was living a lie with his showy form of "manliness," and nobody knew it but him.

When he left the Navy, Alex's confusion caused him to do a dramatic and shocking thing. He had come to the conclusion that the feelings he hid inside were a woman's feelings, not a man's. No "real man" could experience such sensitivity. He decided that he had somehow been born into the wrong body. His identity didn't match his physical design—and he was going to set the situation right. Consequently, Alex denounced his manhood and began the long, complicated process of becoming a woman.

With the help of medical specialists, Alex started a regimen of hormones that would change his appearance and his voice. He began to wear women's clothes, cosmetics, perfumes, and hairstyles. With his doctors' help, he received a new Social Security number, a new driver's license, and every other form of identification necessary to establish himself as a woman—the woman he believed had been trapped inside him, trying to get out for so many years.

On the outside, the transformation process appeared successful. *So why,* Alex asked himself, *after all the work I've done to become the woman I've always dreamed of becoming, am I still so deeply unhappy on the inside?* He had accomplished more than he had ever imagined possible. What was missing?

One night, as this would-be female Alex lay in bed reading, he heard in his spirit words that burned into his soul with their intensity: "Come and drink of the waters of life." Alex knew it was God's voice. Gradually he came to the realization that despite everything he had done to despise the body God had given him, God still loved him.

Even though Alex didn't love himself, God cared enough to reach out and draw him to Himself.

Through the help of a caring Christian friend, and through one of the Dream Center's outreach teams, Alex accepted Jesus Christ as his personal Savior. He repented of his self-deception and his dishonest lifestyle. He returned to his male role, but rejected the false ideas of manhood that had long deceived him. Alex now understands that he doesn't have to be what he describes as a "puffed-up pig of a man"—he left that man in the Navy.

"In Jesus," Alex explains, "I can have a heart, and I can love others openly. Jesus loved, Jesus cried, Jesus cared about others, and He was really a man. I have taken the pain and the confusion and all that made my life hell and I have given it to Jesus, who nailed all of it with His body on His cross. I now know that He loves me, and that He has forgiven me for all that I did. He has given me the strength to face a new life in a new way every day."

A Dream and a Suitcase

LEO PITTS'S GRANDMOTHER TRIED TO WARN HIM THAT LOS Angeles was a corrupt city, but he wanted to go there anyway. He dreamed of leaving the backwaters of Louisiana and beginning a new life in L.A. with his mother and brother. His grandma was just old and worried, he figured. After all, he knew how to take care of himself. And so he headed west.

Leo found a job at a market in Inglewood, near L.A., and he did his work diligently. But it wasn't long before he got mixed up in both drugs and alcohol. He didn't just use drugs; he also sold them. However, since his habit didn't seem to affect his efficiency at work, he assumed he was fine and all was well. He had money, a job, drugs, girls, and whatever else he needed. What did he have to worry about?

Leo juggled his job and his habit for seven years. Eventually, he went to work at another market, where the new owner befriended Leo. The man soon became aware of

Leo's addiction and helped him get into a drug rehabilitation program. For two years Leo was able to kick his own habit, but he continued to make extra money dealing.

At one point the Inglewood police warned him that he would be arrested if he was caught on the streets after 10 P.M. This cramped his style as an after-hours drug dealer, so he moved his business to downtown L.A. Before long he was using drugs again, and his habit was worse than ever. Eventually he quit his job, hit the streets, and began to live in a world of derelicts and Skid Row missions.

One day Matthew invited Leo to get on the bus and go to the Dream Center. Like many others, Leo wasn't so sure that he wanted to go. But when some other street people returned to Skid Row on the white buses and reported how friendly the people at the Dream Center were, he decided to give it a try. What did he have to lose? In fact, when Matthew dared him to get his suitcase and take it with him on the bus, Leo didn't hesitate.

Once at the Dream Center, Leo came to Jesus almost immediately. He went to "The Ranch," a detoxification ministry site, and began an intensive Bible study and discipleship program. There he met his dream girl, Valerie (her story is next). Today they are married and have a beautiful little daughter named Colleen—and Leo is the head of security for the Dream Center.

Leo's joy continues to overflow. "It has been almost three years since Pastor Matthew dared me not only to get my suitcase, but to change my life," he says. "I have a happy family now, and we're just thanking Jesus for everything that we have together!"

A Dream Couple

VALERIE'S EARLIEST YEARS WERE HAPPY, AND SHE STILL remembers enjoying a good life. But when she was barely five years old she was adopted, and that's when the abuse began. She was mistreated, rejected, and betrayed. As the years went by she lost all hope. She dropped out of high school, ran away, and hit the streets—living in cars and sleeping wherever she found a bed. By the time she was eighteen, she was pregnant.

Her daughter was born into an abusive home. The father continually mistreated Valerie and made it impossible for her to properly care for her little girl. Despite her protests, Valerie's parents took custody of the baby, breaking Valerie's heart. It wasn't long before she was pregnant again.

Somewhere along the way Valerie had been introduced to Jesus, and by the time she was ready to deliver her second child, she was living in a Christian home for unwed mothers and had decided to give up her son for adoption. Valerie did well while she was among other believers, but once she left the home where she had been encouraged and cared for, her all-too-familiar patterns of behavior quickly returned.

Valerie made her way to Hollywood where her life became a nightmare of cocaine, marijuana, and prostitution. Lost and alone, she slept in abandoned houses. Once she was arrested for trespassing and tried in vain to explain that she had nowhere else to go. Day-to-day survival became her sole purpose for living. She attempted to stop doing drugs, and she and a friend managed to get an apartment. Old habits prevailed, however, and soon Valerie was back on the streets, without hope or a future.

At about that time, Valerie met a man and woman from the Dream Center who were telling a group of street people about Jesus. She immediately remembered the loving care she had received from Christians when her son had been born. Tired of living such a desperate existence, Valerie accepted the couple's offer of a bed, a meal, and a roof over her head.

At the Dream Center, Valerie didn't have an easy time at first—she says herself that she was a "hard case." Nonetheless, she was loved through her detox program. She was loved through the discipleship program. She was loved so much that eventually she began to believe that God really did have a purpose for her life. She gave her heart to Jesus, once and for all, and this time she didn't look back.

At the Dream Center, Valerie met Leo Pitts. The two fell in love, and with the blessing of Matthew and all the support people who had helped them through the hard times, the two were married. Today Valerie is completing her high-school education and is taking wonderful care of her new daughter, Colleen. "Jesus gave me another gift of being a mother because He has faith in me," she says. "I'm so thankful and enthused because the Lord has made my dream come true."

Empty-Nest Dreamers

DESPITE ALL THE CHALLENGES FACED BY PREACHER'S KIDS, OR "PKs" as they are sometimes called, my children and I have always been the best of friends. Throughout their years of elementary school, junior high, and high school, Luke, Matthew, Kristie, and I did all kinds of things together. We laughed together. We cried together. And we shared the biggest moments of our lives together.

After his high school graduation my oldest boy, Luke, made plans to attend school at Southern California College. It was obvious that our family was about to change forever, and the closer the day of his departure came, the heavier our hearts felt. Matthew and I decided to drive with Luke to Southern California to help him get settled. When the day finally arrived, his mother shed her tears, his sister rejoiced (at least outwardly), and the three Barnett males headed for the coast.

We arrived at the dorm and were just starting to move

Luke's clothes and boxes inside when a young man appeared and introduced himself as Jason, Luke's new roommate. It was wonderful to see the two young men immediately hit it off.

Our plan was to get Luke settled in and then have dinner together at the Red Lion Inn where we had a gift certificate to eat and spend the night. We worked feverishly while the two new roommates continued to talk and get acquainted. Just as we were finishing up, Luke glanced at his new friend, then asked, "Dad, would you feel bad if I stayed here tonight and played basketball with Jason?"

My heart sank. "Oh no, son. Of course not," I said, trying to be big about it. But I felt sick inside. Why was he in such a hurry to get away from his dad and his little brother? "I don't think Luke loves us any more," Matthew moaned as we drove away.

We were both in tears, but we went to the restaurant anyway. Although it was a very fancy place, the elegance was pretty much lost on us. We were too busy talking about Luke to appreciate the lovely table settings and the fine food. We discussed how much we would miss him, and it wasn't long before we were crying again. The waiter listened to us for a few minutes, and by the time we were finished, he was about to cry, too. It was bad enough losing Luke, but far worse was his apparent rejection of us. How could he choose to be with a virtual stranger on the last night the three of us could be together?

We checked into our room, but since it was still early and we were feeling restless, we took a walk around the block. As we walked, we didn't say much—we were feeling weary, bruised, and sad. Then suddenly, around the corner, we saw a young man approaching us. It was Luke! We looked at him in amazement. It seemed that he had been crying, too.

"I got to missing you," he said, "so I came over to say how much I love you."

Matthew and I looked at each other, and we could almost see the heavy weight of sadness lifting from our hearts. Luke still loved us! Everything was going to be all right. In fact, as it turned out, Luke missed us so much that he moved back to Arizona after his freshman year of college. "I just need to be closer to my family," he explained.

A Dream Birthday

DAUGHTERS ARE PRECIOUS TO THEIR DADDIES—MUCH MORE precious than words can say—and from the time my daughter Kristie was a tiny girl, I had a dream developing in my heart for her. This was a dream that I carried with me for years, and one that could only come true at one specific moment in her life. I had decided that when Kristie turned sixteen, I would take her on a very special date—a father-and-daughter date that she would never forget.

As she approached that once-in-a-lifetime birthday, I saved up and planned. And at last the big week arrived.

"Kristie," I told her, "on your sixteenth birthday, you and I are going on a very special date."

Kristie's eyes lit up with excitement. But the closer the actual day came, the more I could tell that my wife, Marja, was feeling a little jealous. She was wondering why she was being left out of all the festivities! It didn't take any thinking at all for me to decide to make it a threesome—Kristie,

115

Marja, and one very proud husband and father.

Weeks before, as a surprise to Kristie, I had scheduled a limousine for the evening. And on Kristie's special day, the beautiful limo drove up and the driver jumped out to open the doors, perfectly dressed in his black suit, cap, and all the trimmings.

"Well," I said to Kristie, "let's go!"

You should have seen her eyes glow! The three of us stepped inside the limo and headed for the best restaurant in town. As we drove, we sipped ginger ale (instead of champagne), celebrating the birth of my only daughter in a style befitting her place in our lives.

My dream present for Kristie Barnett's sixteenth birthday was a night of great joy and revelry. And to this day when she thinks about her birthday, she thinks about Dad. In fact, every time her birthday rolls around now, I have to take her out and buy her a dress. It didn't take much to get her accustomed to the finer things in life!

My son Luke knows he's loved when he's hugged, kissed, and told that he's very dear to my heart. My son Matthew knows he's loved when I spend hours talking to him and interacting about his work, his ministry, and the other things that matter to him.

Kristie appreciates affection, and she values communication. But she really knows she's loved when I take her out and buy her a present. I made doubly sure that she knew how very special she is to me when we shared her dream birthday celebration—a night on the town that none of us will ever forget.

Dreams of Transformation

ROGLIO WAS KNOWN AS THE "GUTTER MAN." HE WAS A Hispanic alcoholic who was also addicted to drugs, and he literally lived in the gutter. He started coming to the Dream Center when he learned that he could get a free meal there, but he didn't stand in line with the other homeless people. "I'm not worthy," he explained. Instead, he made his way to the back door of the kitchen and stood outside, hoping that someone would give him some scraps.

Roglio was probably in his sixties, and his addictions had robbed him of everything he'd ever owned. He had lost his family. He had lost his job. He had lost his possessions. And he had lost his self-respect. If he hadn't been so desperately hungry, Roglio never would have come to the Dream Center at all. But his hunger drew him.

The loving people there began to pray for his salvation and transformation as they awaited his daily arrival. But no matter how much they prayed, Roglio's addiction grew worse. One day he arrived in such a terrible state of intoxication that Margie Watson, who heads up the Dream Center's food ministry, took him in her arms and began to plead with God for his deliverance. One by one, others joined her in her prayer. "Lord, cure him," they cried, "and restore him to genuine life!"

After that scene, Roglio disappeared. The team faithfully prepared his meal every day, but he never showed up to receive it. Margie was particularly worried about him, and as the weeks passed, she continued to pray. At times she feared for his life—he had been so lost and sick. Or maybe he was simply too ashamed ever to return.

Months later Margie was hurrying through the halls of the Dream Center when a man's voice behind her said, "Hello, Margie." She had passed by in a rush, but when she turned around she realized that something about the man was familiar. She stopped and stared.

It was Roglio, but not the same Roglio. This man was clean, carefully dressed, erect, and well groomed. Most noticeable of all, his face was relaxed and peaceful. This new Roglio exuded ease and confidence—entirely unlike the shy, awkward man who had appeared at the kitchen door.

Margie was stunned. "Roglio! What are you doing here?" she exclaimed.

He laughed quietly. "I live here."

"What? Where have you been? I've been so worried!"

Roglio explained that on the very day Margie and the others prayed for him, he had felt something he had never felt before, and he'd asked Jesus to come into his life and save his soul. He had committed himself to the Dream Center discipleship program and was immediately sent to "The Ranch," a detoxification ministry site, where he'd come off drugs and had studied the Bible six hours a day.

Margie's dream came true: Her prayer that Roglio would be transformed was answered. Even now, when the two of them meet in the Dream Center's corridors, they sometimes find themselves in tears—warm tears of gratitude to the Lord, whose love for every person is beyond all measure.

A Homeboy's Dream

MIGUEL COMMITTED HIS FIRST KILLING WHEN HE WAS JUST eight years old. He grew up on the streets—he'd fled there because the violence in his home had been unbearable. And survival on those L.A. streets came down to a simple equation: drugs, murder, and sex. Miguel had already begun drinking alcohol when he took his first hit of heroin at the age of seven. He didn't stop until he was twenty-one.

In the "hood" where Miguel grew up, killing was required of everyone who was initiated into a gang. "My homeboys taught me how to fight," Miguel explains, "and I saw a lot of my homeboys die at my feet and in my arms." Miguel never attended a day of school in his life. His education consisted of learning how to stay alive and how to keep the pain in his heart at bay. Drugs and alcohol dulled the sadness and anger that never left him.

Sometimes Miguel asked God why he couldn't live a "normal" life—playing ball, attending school, dressing up for the prom. But the only answer he could find was written in blood. "Blood in, blood out," as he puts it. The law of the streets was that you had to kill to get in, and if you ever wanted to leave the gang, you were dead. There was no escape—and no future beyond the homeboys and their code.

Miguel had his first major brush with the law at the age of sixteen. "I got caught for killing," he recounts. "I was hanging around with my best friend, and we were barbecuing. Suddenly some dudes passed by in a drive-by, killed my friend's two little kids, and hit my friend in the back, paralyzing him. That was very personal because they were part of my 'family.'

"I went the same night to get the guys who shot my friend, and I made sure they were dead. I was sentenced to fifteen-to-life in the Big House. My lawyer said, 'You've got no hope. What you need is a miracle, not a lawyer.' Right then I hated God."

But God still loved Miguel.

After serving some time in prison, he was released early through a legal technicality. At the time of his release, his mother was working at a clinic, giving shots to some of the people living at the Dream Center. She told Miguel about my son Matthew and the work he is doing in Los Angeles.

Matthew met with Miguel and led him to Christ. After that, everything changed. His life was transformed beyond even his own wildest dreams. "Jesus gave me hope in order to take hope back to the streets of L.A.," he says. "I believe we can reach out to the side of town I grew up in. I believe God is going to do something there—something with me and Matthew."

Dreaming Beyond a Handicap

JIM RITTER, WHOSE BROTHER, DAVID, IS THE MINISTER OF MUSIC at our church in Phoenix, is a living testimony to the way God works in His people's lives to renew their broken and forgotten dreams. Jim and David grew up in the state of Washington, where their father earned his living as a logger. When Jim was sixteen years old, he was ambitious, athletic, and extremely active. Then tragedy struck.

Working for his father's logging company one hot summer day, he decided to take a break after several hours of intensive labor. Dripping with sweat, Jim crawled inside the claw-like grapples that are used to move logs onto trucks. It was cool there, and he cradled himself in the grapples, unaware that his father was about to operate the machinery and pick up a log. All at once he heard the familiar sound, felt the motion—but before he could cry out, it was too late. As the grapples closed, a flash of light pierced Jim's eyes, followed by complete darkness. His father screamed, "Oh, my God! I've crushed him!"

Jim was airlifted by helicopter to a local hospital where the doctors examined him with heavy hearts. Their prognosis was grim: Jim's neck was broken, and he was not expected to live more than a few days.

But the Ritter family believes in prayer, and pray they did, along with their friends and church family. Jim hung on to life by little more than the power of their faith. For a while, all of Jim's vital signs completely stopped except his heartbeat. "He'll be on a breathing machine for the rest of his life," the doctor bluntly informed the Ritter family. "He'll be a head with a stick in his mouth—nothing more than a vegetable."

Upon hearing those cruel words, Jim's father was so overcome with grief that he suffered a near-fatal heart attack himself.

Meanwhile, Jim was given five days to live. But on the fifth day, instead of dying, his organs began to work: Kidneys, bladder, one after the other, function was restored. Little by little, day by day, Jim regained strength, and his prognosis dramatically improved.

At the same time, however, the emotional reality of his paralysis began to sink in. He would never walk again, ride a bike again, or even scratch his nose again. "Lord," Jim prayed, "I know there's a purpose for everything, but I can't see what purpose there could be for me to lie here forever, unable to move."

Over the next few weeks, Jim began to think about heaven, and he remembered Paul's words in Colossians 3:2, "Set your affection on things above, not on things on the earth." He recommitted himself to Christ—just the way he was.

One day a volunteer at his rehab center asked Jim if he wanted to try to paint.

"I can't. I'm paralyzed," he said pointedly, wondering if

she was blind or just not too bright.

The young woman was persistent and showed Jim a drawing made by a paralyzed girl who had learned to hold a pen between her teeth. Since Jim wasn't exactly busy doing other things, he decided to give it a try.

He began slowly, but as the days passed an easily recognizable talent emerged. Before long, his work was breathtaking. Soon he was selling his work, including boxes of Christmas cards with illustrations fashioned from his original paintings.

And another miracle came when Jim and his wife celebrated the birth of their new baby—a baby that doctors had told him would be an impossibility.

Today, nearly twenty-five years later, Jim Ritter gives all the glory to God. "Through my artwork," he says, "God has provided me an opportunity to touch the lives of many others who are discouraged and suffering, both spiritually and physically." Jim travels all over the world giving his testimony and praying for hundreds of other handicapped individuals.

A Dream and a Best Friend

DAN HINZ NEARLY MISSED BEING BORN—HIS MOTHER contracted German measles during her first two months of pregnancy, and almost everyone advised her to have an abortion. Fortunately for Dan, she didn't. But even after that narrow escape Dan's troubles weren't over.

Dan was a drummer in his Southern California high school band, and he fell in love with several Christian music groups. He even asked himself, "Will the Lord find me someday and allow me to play drums for Him in a band?" He dreamed that he could be like them—he actually *prayed* that he could—yet something inside him stubbornly refused to accept Jesus as Savior and Lord. Dan was proud; he didn't want people to see him humbling himself in front of a concert audience, so he refused to go forward at any of the altar calls that always followed his favorite bands' performances.

As he continued to resist Christ, Dan found himself

being drawn ever so gradually into a lifestyle that was anything but Christian. One night in his late teens, Dan was high on drugs and alcohol. As far as he could see, any hope of happiness had passed him by. Gone was his dream of playing Christian music; gone was his prayer for God's touch. His reliance on drugs and booze was eating him alive. Dan wanted to die. In his despair, he stretched his young body across some railroad tracks, hoping a train would end his life instantly. The train came, hit him, and dragged him sixty-two feet. But it didn't kill him.

When the paramedics arrived, Dan was in a coma. His left leg was gone, and part of his right foot was severed. His ear was lying inside the flap of his hat.

Dan survived, but he would be disabled forever.

Some years later, Dan was serving as a live-in babysitter when his dog attacked one of the youngsters in his care. He was grieved to learn that the animal would have to be destroyed. Dan was deeply attached to his dog, and he called a friend in California to tell him of his loss. But Dan's friend didn't want to talk about dogs. Instead, he said, "I know you've been clean and sober for six years, Dan, and you go to Alcoholics Anonymous. That's all good, but try going to church. You need to let Jesus heal your pain."

"You know I don't believe in that Bible jazz!" Dan snapped, slamming down the phone receiver.

A little girl—the sister of the boy who had been attacked by Dan's dog—had been listening. "Dan," she asked innocently, "who were you talking to?"

"That was my best friend," he answered, still annoyed with the conversation.

"He's not your best friend, Dan," she countered.

"Sure he is," Dan responded, somewhat bewildered. "He's the only guy I talk to."

"No, he's not your best friend. Jesus is your best friend."

Dan stared at the child. How could a little kid believe in

Jesus that easily when he couldn't? Dan managed to get himself to church that Sunday. An evangelist was the guest speaker, and Dan looked at him skeptically when he stood up to address the crowd. But the big man had hardly opened his mouth before Dan was in tears. He didn't even wait for the invitation—he rushed down the aisle at the end of the sermon and fell facedown at the man's feet. "I made Jesus my best friend from that day on," Dan says.

And because God remembers our dreams even when we forget them, Dan is now involved in a praise and worship band at our Phoenix church. With a great sense of wonder he joyfully reports that, after all these years, he is finally "making melody" for the Lord (Eph. 5:19). He is currently enrolled in the Pastor's College of Phoenix First Assembly, studying to enter the ministry.

Dreams and God's Presence

DURING MY FIRST PASTORATE IN DAVENPORT, IOWA, I WENT through a period where I profoundly felt that I had lost the conscious presence of God. I was troubled and unsettled. That sort of thing happens to God's people now and then, and I thought I knew what to do: I prayed and fasted. But the sense of loss persisted. For one month I couldn't feel God's presence at all.

I'd stay up all night Saturday night, waiting for God to speak to me about the sermon for the following day. When He didn't instruct me, I'd work over old sermons, recycling them as best I could. People continued to be saved, and the church never ceased to thrive, but I still didn't feel God's presence.

Instead I grew more and more disturbed. God has always known how to get my attention. He knows I'd rather die than lose His conscious presence in my life.

During that dark time I received a call to preach at the

First Assembly of God in Phoenix, Arizona. Known as a "problem church," it had gone through no less than six pastors in ten years—and the current pastor wasn't faring too well, either. Church attendance was down to two hundred people. Now they were inviting me to try out to be their new pastor!

Two hundred people? I thought. *I have four thousand in Davenport. Why would I want to give that up to go to Phoenix?* I set the letter aside.

But as I began to pray, another more important issue pressed to the forefront of my mind. "Whatever it takes to get Your presence back, Lord, that's what I want to do," I prayed.

The Lord spoke to my heart very clearly: "Dig out the letter from Phoenix and go preach to them." God's voice was distinct and His message was indisputable. Obediently, I went to Phoenix and preached to a hundred people.

The service was held in a dark, depressing building. In a way I was relieved to notice only a minimal response to my words; I had no intention of returning there ever again. But on the way back to Iowa, it was as if I heard God say, "If you'll put Me first, I'll return a hundredfold for whatever you give up." He reminded me of Abraham's courageous willingness to sacrifice his only son Isaac.

By now I knew exactly what God wanted. With a heavy heart, but determined to obey, I went back to Davenport and resigned. I was so grieved; I didn't want to leave. But once we moved and I started preaching in Phoenix, things began to happen. The first Sunday many more people came than I expected—six hundred showed up. The next week there were eight hundred, and then there were a thousand. And to this day the ministry in Phoenix has never stopped growing.

Today our annual pastors' and workers' school draws more than seven thousand pastors from across America.

Our weekly television broadcast reaches millions. Our sister church in Los Angeles is multiplying itself with extraordinary speed.

I learned something essential during my temporary loss of God's conscious presence. I discovered that for a dream to be fulfilled, it has to die. That's what the Lord said to me: "Tommy, Abraham gave up his only son—his son of promise. Are you willing to give up your comfortable church in Iowa and step out in faith?"

I said *yes* because I realized that something had to die for my ministry to continue to live. And now, so many years later, I'm still seeing His hundredfold blessing.

A Dream of a New Beginning

JUST A FEW WEEKS AFTER I ARRIVED TO PASTOR THE CHURCH in Phoenix, I found myself going to the church office very early on a wintery Sunday morning. At 5:00 A.M. it was still very dark, and I was in my study, making final preparations for the sermon I would give later that day.

All at once I was startled by a very solid knock on the office door. In those days my door opened onto an inner-city street, and I was a little frightened by the hard, persistent knock. Who was it?

I opened the door, and it was as if my worst fear had become reality. A man bolted in, long-haired, unshaven, and smelling of human waste and alcohol. "Dear Lord," I prayed silently, "what does he want?"

"Mister," the unkempt man said, "I need your help."

Clinging to the belief that God would protect me, I shut the door. "Could you give me some money for food?" the man asked.

I shook my head. "Sir, I'm going to be honest with you. I don't like to give money to people who are going to turn around and spend it on drugs or alcohol. I don't want to contribute to your habit."

He wasn't about to give up. "Mister, I need food. Please help me!"

I studied him for a minute, then I said, "I'll tell you what. If you'll come back to church later on this morning, I'll take you out and buy you something to eat."

He looked down at his pants and shoes. "You don't understand," he explained quietly. "I've messed my pants—can't you smell it? I'm filthy, and I don't have any clothes."

Whatever else he had in mind, he was obviously telling me the truth on that count. "I'll tell you what I'll do," I told him. "I'll drive home, bring you one of my suits, some clean underwear, socks, and whatever else you need." I gave him some soap and showed him where the shower was. Then I drove the seventeen miles to my house and picked out a nice suit—one that I still wore—along with the other essentials. He put them on in my office and left. Honestly, I never expected to see him again.

To my surprise, however, he came to church later that morning, and at the invitation, he came to the altar and accepted Jesus Christ.

Several years later, another young man came to our church. He was the picture of health, a college graduate who had played NCAA football. He became a valuable part of our church family, and eventually a staff member. Years later, we released him to go pastor a church in Detroit. He started with four hundred people in attendance; today he has more than six thousand. His congregation has given more than two hundred thousand dollars to the Dream Center. It's one of the fastest growing churches in America.

Do you know why that wonderful young man came to our church in the first place? He told me one day: "The reason I came here is because you reached out and loved my brother when he was completely unlovable, even to his own family. You gave him a bath, clean clothes, a suit, and most of all, you led him to Christ."

I know I've said it before, but it bears repeating: *Don't be afraid to love the unlovely.* You never know whom you're talking to or what dreams you're setting in motion for the kingdom of God.

Dreamer on a Cross

OUR PHOENIX CHURCH HAS A PROGRAM CALLED "CHURCH ON the Street." Our ministry team goes out into parks and other areas where transients live. A choir sings, a preacher proclaims the gospel, and the team provides a full church service for the homeless and derelict souls who would never find their way into a sanctuary on their own.

One Sunday, Robert was sleeping off a drug binge in a local park. As he awoke, he tried to focus his attention on the gospel message that was being preached nearby. He listened with growing interest as the preacher proclaimed the good news that Jesus could deliver men and women from alcohol and drugs. Robert was not only addicted to both, but he was also in trouble with what he called "the Mob." He needed help in several ways, and what he heard started him wondering: *Could Jesus be the answer to all my problems?*

Robert was as inspired as a man in his situation could be. He got in touch with his sister and asked her if he could live in her home while she helped him "dry out." "There's a church I want to go to on Easter Sunday," he explained with uncharacteristic earnestness. "I think maybe Jesus is the answer for my life." Robert's sister cautiously agreed to help him, and he moved in with her.

On Easter Sunday, Robert arrived at the church early. Just as he walked in the door, a bus full of street people unloaded—a group of homeless men and women who had, at the last minute, agreed to take part in our Easter production and play the role of the "mob" in the Crucifixion scene. When Robert heard the word "mob," he nearly ran away. But before he could, someone mistakenly grabbed him and led him off to the costuming area with the rest of the crowd.

There were several problems with the pageant that Easter. Besides the shortage of "mob" extras, the actor who was supposed to play one of the crucified thieves was sick and didn't show up for his performance. An innovative casting person took one look at Robert and thought he was just the right kind of character. She asked if he would be willing to be hung on a cross during the play. By now Robert was figuring he was having a weird dream of some sort, but he agreed to participate anyway.

Later that morning, as I read the Easter story, I came to the passage about the repentant thief on the cross. Quoting the publican in Luke 18:13, I spoke the immortal words, "God, be merciful to me a sinner."

To my surprise, I heard the same words echoing from one of the crosses on the stage. *"God, be merciful to me a sinner!"* Robert came to church to meet Jesus that Easter Sunday, and he wasn't about to miss the opportunity. Robert was actually saved on that cross, and we prayed with him after the service as he joyfully acknowledged Jesus as Savior and Lord.

Today Robert is part of our church community. He is married to a wonderful woman, and together they are serving the Lord with all their hearts.

A Dream of a Family

As I look across the thousands of faces in our Phoenix congregation, I never really know to whom I may be talking. I have no idea about the untold stories, about the unspoken dreams, about the gains and losses that are concealed behind the smiles and tears I see.

Catherine Share worshiped with us for a long time, but I knew nothing of her past until I ran into her some years later and she finally told me about her life. She was a Jewish Holocaust baby. At three years of age she was hidden in a closet and buried under suffocating piles of clothing while Nazi storm troopers ripped apart the house where she lived. Mercifully, she was spared the concentration camps and soon found a new home across the Atlantic. In America, Catherine was finally safe from the dangers of her early childhood—but the sense of terror never left her.

Years passed, and Catherine grew into an attractive young woman. Like so many others in the 1960s she began to search for a revolutionary experience of love and peace. And like some mysterious fulfillment of her favorite dream, she met a man whose eyes seemed to pierce right through her, penetrating into her need for love. He was strange and unconventional. With words and actions, he convinced her that he would love her and remove the terror from her life. He would provide her with the family she longed for.

The man's name was Charles Manson.

She called him "Charlie," and he called her "Gypsy." So convincing were his lies that his distorted ideas about love made sense to her. Along with his other followers, Gypsy dropped acid regularly, breaking down the boundaries of her personality and, as Manson put it, "deprogramming" her from society. Manson wanted his disciples to empty themselves, to become devoid of ego—to yield their bodies and souls to him.

After the notorious Sharon Tate murders in Hollywood, even after Manson was caught and imprisoned, Gypsy was still devoted to him. Her mind remained twisted by his evil. Although she had not participated in the Tate murders, she had participated in other criminal acts that the "family" committed; eventually she was on the FBI's Most Wanted List.

Gypsy fled to Vancouver, British Columbia, where she tried to start her life over with her son, Paul, who had been fathered by a man who had briefly passed through the Manson family.

"I went into the Manson cult an honest but searching hippie," she says. "I came out a criminal, still loyal to Charlie's causes. I had to get away from Charlie, even if he were God. The life of crime, stealing, lying, conning—my whole life was a lie.

"The gnawing fears Charlie took away returned with a vengeance. He would say that's because I left him. I ached from loneliness, but I couldn't go back. The cure was worse than the disease."

In those days, Gypsy considered folk artist Bob Dylan a "prophet for the times." One day as she heard him sing the popular song "You Gotta Serve Somebody," Catherine realized that she could no longer serve Charles Manson. But whom would she serve now? She returned to the United States with a new question taking form in her mind: *Was Manson really Jesus Christ as he claimed?* Eventually that question was answered.

"The scales fell from my eyes," she remembers. "Jesus did no wrong, yet He took the punishment for every person's wrong. Charlie did wrong all the time and convinced three girls to take his blame. I decided to call on God and ask forgiveness."

Catherine prayed, asked God to forgive her sins, and received Christ. But her troubles weren't quite over. By now the FBI considered Catherine Share the worst con woman in the country. They arrested her, and she served a four-and-one-half-year sentence.

Catherine Share was born into fear and violence, and in her search to fulfill her dreams of family and security, she became entangled in the worst nightmare imaginable. Today she is a redeemed, productive member of society. She has found a family, both with her husband and son, and with the family of God. God delivered her from many of her fears. She is still working through a lingering phobia with the help of God, trusting in Christ's covering of love, mercy, and forgiveness.

"If it covers me," she'll tell you with a smile, "it can cover anyone who accepts Him."

Resurrected Dreams

BY THE TIME I MET CATHERINE SHARE SHE WAS IN THE PROCESS
of telling her story to a writer who had agreed to help create
a book about her testimony. In the process of working with
Catherine, Janna Hughes had a dramatic experience of her
own—and it nearly stopped her writing career in its tracks.

Janna was an award-winning producer when a dream
first emerged in her mind. Although she was successful, she
felt an emptiness in the work she was doing, and deep in
her soul she dreamed of accomplishing something more
meaningful. She began to envision a series of entertaining,
true stories about people whose lives had been changed forever by an encounter with Jesus.

At the time, Janna was making most of her money on
commercials and industrial videos. But believing God had
given her the dream, she committed herself to it and
decided to step out in faith and watch how He would bring
it to pass. She resolved not to undertake any new projects

that would interfere with the inspiring films and videos she wanted to produce for Him.

Then one Sunday, everything changed. Driving home from church, Janna barely noticed a speeding car hurtling out of a side street. "All I saw was a red streak," she remembers, "and when my car stopped spinning, I didn't know how to walk."

Unfortunately, Janna's injuries were not visible to the paramedics. They took her to a local hospital instead of to a trauma center. Since she did not appear to be bleeding or have any other telltale signs of internal injury, the emergency room team sent her home five hours later. But on the inside of Janna's head, all was not well. Later, when she was correctly diagnosed, she learned that she had suffered internal injuries, damage to the left inner ear, and brain trauma. As far as the brain injury was concerned, there was no prognosis for recovery.

Janna was in a fog, baffled and confused. Deep questions haunted her: *How does a person who was once a writer/producer, who had a sharp mind for detail and an ability to handle the related stress, accept that she doesn't know what year it is five minutes after being told? How does a person with newly acquired learning disabilities prepare for the future—when she's a single mom and the sole support of the household?*

"My inability to handle the simplest tasks of life made me question why God left me in such a state," she says. "Each dawn brought to light the same hopeless situation. I wanted to die."

Janna's nausea and dizziness were so acute that she hardly left the house. Her life became limited and reclusive; depression and despair were her constant companions. Through treatment with a neurologist and cognitive rehabilitation with a neuropsychologist, she gained some understanding of her condition and the task that lay before her. But life was almost too much to bear. The poster beside her computer said it all: "Due to financial constraints, the light at the end of the tunnel will be turned off until further notice."

One day Janna lay in bed with the blinds drawn, her head wracked with pain as it often was. Even a hint of light made the pain worse. Lying there with her eyes closed, she wondered what she could possibly do with her life. A moment later, she knew. She could pray. It dawned on her that she could impact lives, neighborhoods, even cities through the power of prayer.

That satisfied her. "If I could never reenter society," she says, "if I had to continue to live like a hermit, I could still pray. If I could do nothing but pray for the remainder of my life, that would be enough."

Eventually, inner ear surgery corrected some of the problems that kept her at home, and she started going out again. One day she attended a women's meeting at a new church. The leader (who knew nothing about Janna's condition, much less the poster on her wall) began to speak powerful words of spiritual encouragement: "It's like you've been in a dark tunnel, a very dark place," she told her. "Get ready; the light is coming on at the end of the tunnel."

Today, slowly but surely, Janna is writing again. Methodically she wends her way through the myriad problems related to brain and memory impairment, which have affected her daily life, writing, and production. But at a snail's pace, her progress continues. She is putting together a documentary of her personal odyssey—the true story of her own encounter with Jesus in the face of tragedy. She believes it will be the first of those real-life Christian stories she dreamed of producing before the accident.

"Now I know that God chose me to do a certain thing," Janna explains. "Although I am never expected to be the same, whatever is lost in me God doesn't need. I'm His chosen vessel, and He will work through me until the dream is fulfilled."

A Threatened Dream

MY FATHER WAS A GIFTED EVANGELIST, AND FROM AN EARLY age he dreamed of reaching his world for Christ. He preached on street corners, held meetings on courthouse steps, and visited churches and schools with the gospel message. He didn't make much money, however, so my mother and I went to live with my grandparents in Texas while he held revivals across several Midwestern states.

One night my mother urgently called him in Granite City, Illinois. "Come home quickly, honey!" she said. "Tommy is dying! The doctor says he has double pneumonia, and he can't get his breath. Will you come?"

Dad sank into a chair and closed his eyes. There in Granite City, for the first time, he was seeing truly dramatic results from his preaching. Already ninety people had come to Christ, and the bartenders in town were complaining about lost business. What's more, that very day the pastor of the church where the revival services were being held had asked Dad if he would stay an extra week and continue the revival.

"Honey," he told my mother, his heart aching with sadness, "I don't want to sound cruel. But I don't know if it is God's will for me to come home right now."

My mother begged him, then put Dad's mother on the phone. My grandmother minced no words: "Son, don't you love your own son? Don't you care anything about him? If you care about him, you'll come home right now." She paused. "Herschel! Will you come home?"

Dad wiped his eyes wearily. "Don't make me answer now," he said. He hung up the phone, got on his knees, and wept. "God, not my will but Thine be done," he prayed. "Let my actions be Thy actions."

He waited, still kneeling, to hear God's reply. After a while God spoke to his heart some words that he would never forget: "You put My work first, and I'll take care of your work. You put My things first, and I'll take care of your things."

Dad called Texas. "Joy, I'm sorry," he told my mother. "I love you and Tommy so much. But I've got to stay here. God has work for me to do here and now. And I have to stay and do it."

Dad received more than one telegram in the days that followed, and from what he read, it sounded like I was on my way to eternity—it was just a matter of time. He was painfully torn, wondering if he'd made the right decision. Would I die without my daddy there to comfort me? Would my mother ever forgive him?

With a heavy heart, Dad continued preaching, and God graciously brought hundreds of souls to faith that week. The instant he finished his final sermon on Sunday, he jumped into his car and drove night and day until he reached Texas. When he pulled up to the house, he saw the family doctor backing out of the driveway, shaking his head.

143

Terrified, Dad jumped out of the car and flung open the front door. There I was, crawling across the floor, my cheeks pink and my smile in place. My mother was smiling, too. "The doctor says it's nothing short of a miracle," she said.

You see, at the very moment my father finished his last sermon in Granite Falls, his unconscious baby boy abruptly woke up and his breathing returned to normal. I was suddenly, unexplainably well again.

From that moment on a great change occurred in my father's ministry. Never before had God so richly blessed his efforts. Dad always explained it by saying that he had proven to God that His work came first. After that, God took care of everything else.

My Dad and Oral Roberts's Dream

ONE DAY I RECEIVED AN UNEXPECTED PHONE CALL FROM A MAN I'd always admired. When I first heard him say *hello*, I knew his voice sounded familiar. He didn't keep me guessing for long. "This is Oral Roberts calling you from Tulsa," he said. "I've been watching you on television, and your message— 'Find a need and fill it; find a hurt and heal it'—appeals very much to me."

"I'm glad to hear that . . ." I began.

But Dr. Roberts wasn't finished. "You said something else," he told me. "You said, 'Whatever you want in life, you've got to give it away to get it.' Do you remember saying that?"

"Yes, sir. I've said it often, and I believe it with all my heart."

"Well, would you come and spend a day with me?" Oral Roberts asked. "I need to talk to you."

Of course I was greatly honored by his request, and as

145

soon as possible, I flew to Tulsa. Before long I found myself sitting in his expansive office in the tallest skyscraper in Oklahoma.

"I've built a big hospital here," Oral Roberts said quietly, "but I'm having a hard time filling it with people. After hearing what you had to say the other night, I've decided that I want to open the City of Faith to anyone who wants to come for treatment—even those who can't afford it. I want to provide rooms and care free of charge."

I thought it was wonderful idea, and I felt deeply honored to have had some part in the decision. Once that issue was settled, we continued to chat. It was a very inspirational time for me. At one point he asked me where I grew up.

"I'm from Kansas City," I answered.

He paused for a moment, then a look of recognition brightened in his eyes. "Barnett? Barnett! Did your dad pastor a church in Kansas City fifty years ago?"

"Yes, he did. He pastored there for forty years."

"Was he a short man, around five foot eight, weighing about two hundred thirty pounds?"

"Yes, that was definitely my dad. But why do you ask?"

"Oh, I remember your dad very well," Oral Roberts told me, tears filling his eyes. "Years ago I went to Kansas City with a group of pastors to see about holding a citywide revival there. We ended up in a very unpleasant meeting. The local pastors didn't like our idea at all. There were verbal attacks against us. It became so intense that I even thought some of those men would attack me physically. I was afraid."

He paused, looking out over the city for a moment as he recalled the unpleasant incident. Then he continued. "Your dad stood up, walked toward me, and stood directly in front of me. He literally shielded me from the others. He told them what our crusade would be like, how it could take place, and what a blessing it would be. And he turned the tide. Then and there, everyone decided to cooperate. Your dad helped me make my dream come true."

I wasn't surprised to hear about Dad's response—it sounded just like him. But I'd never heard about the incident, and I told Oral Roberts so.

"Well, it was a long time ago, and I haven't seen your father since. But I'd like to do something in honor of what he did for me. At this school, we give honorary doctoral degrees. Would you permit me to give you an honorary doctorate to honor both you and your father?"

Later on that spring, with thousands of students and parents looking on, I was given a doctoral degree from Oral Roberts University. Academically, I didn't qualify for that credential at all. But I got it anyway—through the faithfulness of my daddy.

The Bible says that the "iniquities of the fathers" can have a negative impact upon three or four generations of descendants (Exod. 20:5). But it also says that the benefits of righteousness can carry on for thousands of generations later (Ps. 106:31). My father's goodness brought me a unique and treasured reward, and Dad's foundation—the Word of God—continues to form the bedrock beneath my ministry and my sons' ministries, too.

A Rainy Day Dreamer

A MISSIONARY IN A PHILIPPINE JUNGLE TOWN ASKED ME TO come and preach the gospel. I was used to traveling internationally, but as I made my way to that particular town I encountered some unusual obstacles. The only way into the area was by boat, so for several hours we threaded our way through white water rapids in not-so-sturdy canoes. It was a long, wet journey, and when we finally arrived, we found ourselves face to face with one worried missionary. It had been raining all day, and he wondered what kind of a crowd we would attract.

During a break in the clouds we set up our lights in the town square. Before we were finished, however, it was drizzling again. The missionary glared at the sky and sighed wearily. We decided to start the music anyway. Amazingly, the more we sang, the more the clouds parted; the more the clouds parted, the more people showed up.

Feeling more confident, I began to preach. But the

minute I started, the town's cathedral bells on the other side of the square pealed out with an almost deafening sound. I hesitated, and then continued; I then started and stopped again. The bells kept ringing for fifteen minutes. Finally I heard a wonderful, peaceful silence. My gospel message soared, and the audience listened wholeheartedly.

Then the rain began again.

This time it was no drizzle. It was one of those tropical rainstorms where the sky opens up and water gushes out in bucketsful. In seconds I was soaked to the skin. I sadly looked out on the people facing me, clothes drenched and their hair dripping down in their eyes. I noticed one young woman leaving the crowd and whispering something to the missionary. The missionary in turn walked up to me and said, "They want you to go on. Don't stop."

So I finished my message. When I gave the invitation, a young man rushed to the front, tears mingling with the raindrops on his face. "I would never have seen your Jesus if you had not described Him to me the way you did tonight," he said. "Now I understand, and I will be faithful to Him always. You will see. You will see."

A few days later we held one final, dynamic rally in Manila's Bethel Temple. After the service someone tapped me on the shoulder. I was surprised to find myself standing face to face with the young man who had given his life to Jesus that rainy night.

"When did you come to Manila?" I asked him.

"I came tonight. I walked all the way."

I stared at him in disbelief. "That's over a hundred miles!"

"I know," he replied. "But I want you to know that I mean business about following Jesus. I want to serve Him in my country. And I wanted to thank you for coming to my town and telling me about Him."

I thought back on the difficulties we'd faced in holding that meeting and breathed a silent prayer of thanks that we hadn't given up and walked away. There stood the first fruits of my message!

"Jesus is the One who sent me," I told that determined young man, feeling very humbled and grateful. "He's the One who brought me here. Whatever you do, don't forget to thank Him."

Dreams and Headhunters

AFTER HOLDING A SERIES OF SUCCESSFUL EVANGELISTIC crusades in the Philippines, I returned at the request of a missionary who wanted me to preach to a group of aboriginal tribesmen. The missionary was determined to reach one particular tribe of headhunters who had never seen a white man before. In fact, the headhunters, who were known for their fierce warfare tactics, lived in such a remote area that they had never even seen some of the other indigenous tribes in the surrounding mountains. They were still known for taking the heads of neighboring tribesmen.

Our trip had been carefully planned, and we had hired a big van to carry our gear along with salt, dolls, toy trucks, and an assortment of other gifts to present to the tribal chief as tokens of our friendship. We were very enthusiastic about our adventure, knowing that this group was one of the last tribes on earth that had never heard the gospel.

The road leading part of the way into the area where

this tribe lived led through a mountainous region where a faction of communist rebels was known to hide out. It was very rough country, and the communists who lived there wreaked havoc and destruction upon anyone who encountered them. We were told to be careful and, above all else, to avoid blockades. If we hit a roadblock, we were warned, we would be robbed and probably killed.

The muddy road curved treacherously, dropping off more than a thousand feet straight down on one side. We drove slowly, watching out for danger of every kind. All at once, we came upon a bus that was turned upside down.

"Watch out!" said the missionary to the driver. "It could be a raid."

The driver threw the van in reverse and began to turn around. But before he could move, several wild-looking people jumped out from behind the bus, terrified, and ran in our direction. Blood poured out of their faces, arms, and legs. There had been a terrible accident, and the bus had rolled over several times. One man looked as if he'd been scalped. Another's leg was almost entirely ripped off, held in place by only a small piece of skin. A woman screamed, "My son is in there. See if he's okay!"

Gasoline streamed out from under the bus, which was ready to explode at any moment. Somehow I made my way inside the overturned vehicle by crawling through a window. As I removed one sack of rice after another, I came upon a pair of hands. I felt for a pulse, but there was nothing—the woman's son had been crushed to death under the weight of several heavy rice sacks that were being taken to market.

Without further discussion we aborted our visit to the headhunters' tribe, and, with every seat in our van filled with wounded people, we headed back down the mountain as fast as we could. I hadn't noticed how bumpy the road was on the way up; now the injured cried out in agony as we hit pothole after pothole.

The missionary looked around the bus with tears in his eyes. "Tommy," he said, "the spiritual condition of these people is worse than their physical condition. Let's tell them about Jesus."

Breathing a quick prayer for God's help, I turned and looked gently at those battered faces. With the missionary interpreting, I started, "Some of you may not make it to the hospital, so I want to make sure that you make it to heaven. . . . " By the time I finished, everyone on the bus had accepted Christ. And all but one of them lived.

A few weeks later, the missionary learned that one of those injured people was the mayor of one of the largest villages in that part of the country. Deeply moved by the accident and our help, he invited the missionary to come to his village to tell all his people about Jesus Christ. Most of the villagers accepted Jesus Christ as their personal Savior as a result of his visit. We missed our dream of going to the tribe of headhunters—the missionary finally got there some years later—but God worked everything out for the best, and with His help, new dreams were born.

Dreams on Wheels

SICK OF FIGHTING WITH HIS FATHER, RANDY FIKES LEFT home at thirteen years of age. Rebellion raged within him, and he was eager to experience life on the streets where the alcohol and drugs he was already using were more readily available. It wasn't long before he was sleeping in parks, on benches, under trees, or in doorways. It wasn't much of a life, and eventually he decided that since he didn't have a home anyway, he might as well go where the action was. He headed for California.

In San Diego, Randy got into a knife fight, which severely damaged his throat. Then, fleeing a world of trouble, he found his way to Phoenix. There he was attacked from behind by an unknown assailant, who beat him viciously and left him for dead. The medical experts who handled Randy's case determined that he was a lost cause—if he ever came out of his coma, he would have no bodily functions left. Essentially, they said, he would be a vegetable.

Randy was placed in long-term care at a series of convalescent homes. It was from one of those Phoenix hospitals that he was picked up by our wheelchair-access church bus as it picked up people from nursing homes to attend church services. Randy was perfectly happy to get out of the hospital and visit the church where he met new friends and saw so many attractive young women. I can still remember the way his face lit up at the sight of a pretty girl!

Randy tried to talk but he was unable to do so, despite his valiant efforts to communicate. He tried to walk too, but to no avail. Still he was undaunted, finding pleasure in taking special care of the people who rode his bus, attempting to let the driver know if someone was unable to attend.

One Sunday—to the amazement of everyone who saw it—Randy put down his cane, raised his hands, and with tears pouring down his cheeks and with no help from anyone, he walked to the altar to accept Jesus as his Savior. He was baptized, and from that point on his condition continued to improve.

A bus pastor who had been carefully monitoring Randy's progress asked him one day if he would like to work on his speech. He beamed with pleasure and hope. "It's not going to be easy," the pastor told him, "but let's see what we can do."

With index cards and countless hours of effort, he mastered a number of words. New sets of cards were made, and every two or three weeks Randy learned all the words in each new set. After developing a usable vocabulary, Randy began to memorize Scripture. Then he decided he wanted to learn to write. In everything he tried, his progress was remarkable.

One of the high points of Randy's new life came when he was able to travel to Detroit to visit family members—people who had given up on him long before. It was after one of those Christmas trips that Randy fell ill and died. His family members came to the funeral at our church, which was a celebration of his amazing new life in Christ. Before they left Phoenix they asked the Lord to come into their lives, too.

As it turned out, Randy was more than victorious over his handicaps. He was determined and diligent, dedicated to finding new dreams and making them come true. Most important of all, even in death, Randy Fikes was a soul-winner, too.

A Young Mother's Dream

WHEN ASHLEY TOLD HER STORY, EVERYONE LISTENED carefully. Unlike so many young people who find themselves on the streets while still in their teens, Ashley grew up in wealth and privilege. Her father was an international executive, and her mother was listed in the social register, well known in circles of charity work and exclusive women's clubs. As a child, Ashley had it all—everything, that is, except love.

Like many young women Ashley's search for love led her astray, and by the time she was sixteen, she was pregnant with the child of a boy she hardly knew. Her parents were appalled. What would the community think? They demanded that she have an abortion; when she refused, they kicked her out of their house and out of their lives. She had no money, no place to live, and no idea what to do or where to go.

Ashley came to our church's ministry for unwed mothers,

which is called "His Sheltering Wing." The first thing our counselors did was introduce Ashley to Jesus and assure her that she would never again be alone or unloved. Then they began the practical process of teaching her how to care for herself and her unborn child, helping her review the alternatives she faced once her baby was delivered.

Ashley wholeheartedly decided to keep her baby.

All her life Ashley wanted to live in a family where love was the first priority. Today she is making her dream come true in the life of her little son. In the process she has never shrunk back from hard work—and it has been hard at times. But by the time she was twenty years old, besides being a proud mother, she had bought her own house, leased her own car, and was able to tithe to the church, in addition to providing a comfortable, godly home for her baby.

"I never take anything for granted," she smiles, "especially the love of God that was showered on me through the wonderful people at His Sheltering Wing. They took me in. They introduced me to Jesus. And they demonstrated a better way to live, better than anything I'd ever known before."

Beyond His Wildest Dreams

JACOB CAME TO OUR CHURCH IN SEARCH OF A CHRISTIAN community that could help him struggle through his battle with AIDS. Already sick with some fairly serious symptoms, he had turned his back on his former life as a homosexual and was now reaching out for Christian support. Unfortunately, some other churches hadn't been especially glad to see him. Many Christians are unsure what their role should be in the face of homosexuality and AIDS, and, rather than reach out, they simply withdraw. Thankfully, even though Jacob was rejected again and again by Christians, he never lost his faith in God.

Jacob became a part of our AIDS ministry, and as he waited, along with the others, for the virus to gradually wreak havoc with his body, he continued to fellowship with the other AIDS victims at our church. Then one day he became quite sick. Although he knew he was dealing with an unrelated illness, he realized how important it was to get immediate medical attention. Praying for God's help, he rushed to the doctor.

The doctor knew all about Jacob's HIV-positive condition and took a series of routine blood tests. As he evaluated the results, he was confused. Without explaining why, he asked Jacob to come back in for further tests.

"What's going on?" he asked another doctor as he studied the results of the blood test. Impossible as it seemed, there was no trace of the AIDS virus in Jacob's body! Even more amazing, his T-cell blood count was above normal.

Today Jacob can't stop talking about Jesus. "I was diagnosed as 'hopeless,' and yet today I'm filled with hope," he says. "I am so grateful to be a witness of the living miracle the Lord Jesus has worked in my life. I was an outcast and a sinner, filled with faults, but God saw me complete and whole through His Son Jesus. What He's done for me goes beyond my wildest dreams."

Dreams and Deacons

As a small boy, my family and I lived in a church parsonage. In those days, we still celebrated Halloween very innocently—nobody had yet told us that it was the devil's holiday. So, since we didn't know any better, I always had a jack-o'-lantern. One Halloween night before I went to church, a friend and I were admiring my little cardboard jack-o'-lantern.

Just as my friend left, he said, "You'd better blow out the candle. If you don't, you'll burn the house down!" Naturally I was going to blow the candle out. In fact I sincerely thought that I did. But there's a good chance I didn't.

While we were in church that Wednesday night, we heard a fire truck's siren getting closer and closer. Then Dad's sermon was abruptly interrupted when a man rushed in shouting, "The parsonage is on fire!"

We all scrambled outside, and we watched in horror as an inferno nearly destroyed our home. After the fire was extinguished, the firemen began to look for possible causes. They said it was one of two things: Either something had caught on fire on top of the chest of drawers (which is where I had placed the jack-o'-lantern), or it started in the wiring.

My friend who had been admiring my jack-o'-lantern earlier said, "Tommy, I *told* you to blow out the candle!" He looked around and repeated to the others, "I told him to blow it out!"

My heart sank. With a terrible, guilty feeling I listened while my dad talked to the deacons. One of those deacons was very emphatic. He spoke up boldly, and he said, "It was the wiring—no question about it! That wiring has been bad for years. It's our fault! We should have taken care of it a long time ago."

The others nodded. My friend shrugged and left with his parents. And those wonderful deacons chose to believe it was the wiring—not the jack-o'-lantern. My little heart was touched—I had been scared to death, and those good men had saved my neck.

I always smile when people say, "You sure do love your deacons, don't you?" I do love deacons, and I'll tell you why. My dad's deacons were once very kind to a frightened little boy who may—or may not—have burned down the church parsonage!

Secret Dreams

I HAVE NEVER TOLD THIS STORY—BUT I DO SO NOW BECAUSE I believe it might help another young minister who may feel as I once did. All my life I've been involved with Assemblies of God churches. My dad was an Assemblies of God preacher, and the heroes of my life have always been pastors and missionaries of that great denomination. Even as a boy, I attended our denomination's General Council with my family every year. We never missed it.

For years my dad pastored the largest Assemblies of God church in the country. But his church was different from many others.

One day a man introduced himself to Dad. He pointed toward a run-down vehicle parked at the curb and said, "Can you use this bus?" Dad accepted the donation and used it to launch his bus ministry—picking up the kind of kids nobody wanted and bringing them to church. Eventually that one vehicle became a fleet of buses. Church volunteers went out on each bus route, knocked on doors, and invited as many children to church as the buses would hold. Herschel Barnett's bus ministry exploded.

Now there were a few people in our denomination who made fun of Barnett and the "bus kids." But kids eventually grow up. It's true that nobody wanted those boys and girls when they were small, but forty years later, those "bus kids" became Dad's deacons and church leaders. In the meantime, though, Dad wasn't always as respected as he should have been, despite his huge church.

Because some of the denominational leadership saw Dad in that negative light, he was never asked to speak at big gatherings or at the District Council—much less at the General Council. As a boy that bothered me, and I developed a tinge of resentment toward those leaders. Today I can say that my attitude was wrong, but I have to admit that's how I felt back then.

When I went to build my own church in Davenport, Iowa, history seemed to repeat itself. My church soon became the fastest-growing church in America. Yet during the planning of the first Assemblies of God church-growth conference, the denominational leadership invited a number of speakers who pastored thriving congregations—but they didn't invite Tommy Barnett.

People called in to ask, "Why isn't Tommy Barnett speaking?" Succumbing to the pressure, the leaders called me and said, "We want you to speak at a big breakfast." Although I didn't really feel accepted, I agreed to speak to those three thousand pastors. But I knew the breakfast meeting had been added on as an afterthought, and it didn't improve my attitude.

As the years passed, I was still not invited to speak at any national conference. In my resentment I told my family privately, "Someday I may be invited, but I'm not going to speak. They have never appreciated Dad and me." By then I had a big church filled not only with bus kids, but also with wealthy people. But I also had bitterness in my heart. Again, in retrospect, I can see that others were not at fault—*I* had a weakness, and it was causing me great pain. It felt like an open wound.

Then one day I received a letter from the General Council inviting me to be one of the speakers at the next conference, which would be held in the gigantic domed stadium in Indianapolis. It would be the largest gathering the Assemblies of God had ever held. To be honest, I never thought they'd ask me. But by the time I got the letter, God had been doing an important work in my heart. I remembered my vow to my family—that if I were ever asked, I would refuse to speak. But I had come to see that my motivation had been wrong all along. I would say *no*, but not out of resentment.

I wrote a letter declining the invitation to speak in Indianapolis. I explained that there were two reasons. First, I had long held wrong feelings in my heart against the denominational leadership because I felt my father and I had been overlooked. Second, I needed to get my heart purified. Then I asked them for forgiveness. "I am not worthy to speak in Indianapolis because of an attitude that I've kept inside for a long time," I wrote. "Please forgive me."

I went on my way. Four years later, the Assemblies of God wrote to me again. This time they asked me to speak in Portland, Oregon. By then I had the proper motivation. God had done the purification work I'd asked Him to do. It was no longer even important to me that I be asked to speak, but the fact that they valued me touched me deeply. And by then I understood that everybody couldn't be invited to speak at every event. I accepted the invitation, and it turned out to be one of the most wonderful preaching experiences I've ever had. It was also at that conference that my son Matthew was called to preach the gospel.

Several more years passed, and there came an even greater honor. I was nominated by the District Council to serve as Executive Presbyter for the Assemblies' Southwest region. Ironically, I didn't know about the nomination. Traditionally, nominees are always notified. But somehow the communication wires got crossed, and everybody assumed someone else had told me.

One day a friend said, "You didn't tell me you were running for Executive Presbyter."

"I'm not," I told him.

"Oh, yes, you are."

I called our District Superintendent and learned that my friend was right. I probably would not have allowed my name to be on the ballot if I had been aware of the nomination. For one thing, by then I was far too busy to serve in such a key position. For another, I didn't think in a million years that I would ever be elected. I couldn't imagine being one of fourteen men who make policy for a denomination responsible for thirty million souls around the world!

In spite of everything I was elected, and for two years I served my denomination in this wonderful position until my schedule made it impossible for me to continue. That two-year leadership experience did more for me than I ever could have foreseen. The Assemblies of God helped make my secret dreams come true—dreams that I had even kept secret from myself: dreams of being accepted, honored, and loved.

Today in my office there hangs a picture of me preaching to a capacity crowd in Portland, Oregon. That Portland event was a turning point in my life. I will always appreciate my friends and colleagues in the Assemblies of God for giving me time to grow up, for believing in me, and for making my dreams a reality.

Dreams of Joy

MY MOTHER, JOY, ALWAYS DREAMED OF THE DAY I WOULD bring home a bride for her to love, and she was praying for my future wife before I ever thought about having one. Little did she know that my wife-to-be would be born halfway around the globe into the worst imaginable circumstances.

Marja came into the world in Finland. Her father died in military service, and her mother was poverty-stricken. To make matters worse, the little girl's grandmother was a desperate alcoholic who sent Marja's mother out into prostitution to pay for her habit. A sickly little girl, Marja was plagued with respiratory illness, ate out of garbage cans, and was shuttled from one orphanage to another.

She finally ended up in Sweden, adopted by a loving Swedish family. Although the family was not Christian, they were kind to their new daughter and met many of the needs of her young life. But her adoptive mother taught

Marja something very strange, and she stressed it without fail: "You will marry someday, and when you do, *never trust your mother-in-law*. Mothers-in-law are dangerous and wicked, and they always cause pain."

When I met Marja (that story comes next), I invited her to spend three months with my parents. We both understood that eventually I hoped to make her my wife. But her hopeful journey to Kansas City to my parents' home was shadowed by her lifelong fear. My mother was probably her future mother-in-law. Would she really be as evil as Marja had been told?

One thing was missing from Marja's adoptive family, and that was the Lord. His love, guidance, and protection had never been demonstrated to her even though she had attended a Lutheran church. She could not imagine a family like ours, where God's goodness was ever present. Marja couldn't comprehend a home where God had placed His own deep love in the hearts of each family member and where God had a warm welcome prepared for Marja before she ever arrived.

Despite Marja's initial uncertainty, the two women quickly learned to love each other. And the most astounding coincidence began to reveal itself. My mother and my fiancée were very much alike, to the point of sometimes buying the same items at the store when they shopped independently. Even our family doctor declared that I had chosen a "mother image" for a wife. Today these two women are like mother and daughter. Marja says that Joy is no longer her mother-in-law; she has become her mother-in-*love*.

Joy's dream of a lovely daughter-in-law came true in Marja. And Marja's fear of an evil mother-in-law was forever banished by the loving, kindred spirit she found in Joy Barnett.

A Dream of a New World

MY WIFE'S EARLY YEARS WERE MARRED BY PAIN AND SICKNESS, neglect and poverty. Even after being rescued from Finland's streets and placed in a series of orphanages, she was terrified and unable to reach out in love. Yet, as she says, "The Lord had a plan for my life." I'll let Marja tell the story of her dream of coming to America in her own words, and how that dream came true—God's way:

"As a child I attended Lutheran services with my mother, but they were not especially meaningful to me. However, I deeply understood the importance of a little crucifix that hung on the wall of my bedroom. Somehow I knew that the Man on that cross loved me and would take care of me.

"When I reached young womanhood, I was a model for clothing and hair designs, and I had even been asked to participate in the Miss Sweden Beauty Pageant. My life was full, exciting, and rich in promise. But there was a deep emptiness in my spirit.

"In search of fame and fortune, a girlfriend and I decided to go to America when I was in my early twenties. I guess we thought we would marry millionaires and live happily ever after. But my heart wasn't entirely frivolous. One day, just before we left Sweden on our journey, I stood thoughtfully before the crucifix on my wall. In a moment of sincere prayer, I asked God for help, guidance, and protection.

"When we boarded the plane for the United States, my friend and I were dressed in our finest suits and hats, and we turned several heads as we made our way to our seats. Throughout the trip, people paid a lot of attention to us. We felt like mysterious film stars, and we allowed our admirers to think that we were on our way to Hollywood in pursuit of glamorous careers. Little did they know that we would soon be working as maids and au pairs!

"We hadn't been in Palo Alto, California, a week when I met an interesting new friend. She called herself a 'born-again Christian' and insisted on taking me with her to some sort of religious meeting at her church. It turned out to be a revival meeting, and the evangelist's name was Tommy Barnett!

"My English wasn't the best, and I found it hard to follow what the young man was saying. But something drew me back to that same church the following night. And when I went up to the altar at the end of the service to accept Jesus Christ as my Savior, Tommy Barnett was there to meet me at the front and pray the sinner's prayer with me. I could not have imagined it at the time, but just three months later I became his wife.

"My early years had not prepared me to be warm or affectionate. I was not comfortable in expressing love and was very self-protective. My husband was my teacher in so many ways—he helped me learn to receive love as well as to give it. His Christlike example helped me understand that loving requires vulnerability and that my self-protectiveness would never allow me to give my heart to others.

"How grateful I am for the leading of God! He answered the simple prayer that I prayed in my room so long ago. He has guided me, protected me, and helped me all the years of my life. I am truly rich in Him and in His love for me."

Helping Others Dream

DID YOU KNOW THAT YOU CAN BE JUST AS CLOSE TO A PERSON you admire as you want to be? I once heard a well-known pastor say, "Two objects don't need to move—only one does. I can stand as close to this pulpit as I want to. All I have to do is walk toward it, and the steps I take are the only ones that matter."

We often feel close to important people in high places, whether they are presidents, fine musicians, or athletes we admire. For example, when I heard that Bo Jackson wanted to play baseball, not football, I was impressed, because I knew that he could have made much more money playing football. I admired him so much for pursuing his dream—it encouraged me to pursue some dreams of mine. I decided that he was going to be friend. Now Bo Jackson has no idea that I'm his friend, but I am his friend anyway.

I feel the same way about Ronald Reagan. I consider myself his friend, even though he's not aware of our friendship. His ability to dream and make dreams become reality has been a source of inspiration for me.

One day after church, an elderly lady walked slowly up to me and shook my hand. And she said something I'll never forget. "I was here when you came to Phoenix," she told me. "I've been in this church for eighteen years. I've never shaken your hand before because so many people need your time. But I'm eighty-five years old, Preacher, and you are the closest friend I have in the entire world! I feel so close to you. I've been stuck in the snow listening to your sermons. I've brushed my teeth with you. I've cooked my dinner with you. I've even taken a shower with you! (Remember, she was eighty-five years old!) I want to thank you—because you have become my closest friend."

I was so touched by her words. She helped me understand that when you help people dream, you become their friend for life. And you can do that through the power of identification—whether or not they ever meet you face to face.

A Dream Delayed

ONE OF THE MOST IMPORTANT LESSONS WE CAN LEARN ABOUT dreams is that they don't always come true right on time. That doesn't mean they'll never come true. And it doesn't mean there's something wrong with them. It just means that God's view of timing is sometimes very different than ours.

One of the dreams I had when I first moved to Phoenix was to build a simple little prayer chapel on a mountainside. I envisioned it surrounded by natural growth in a garden designed by the hand of God. I thought it would be wonderful if people could pray there twenty-four hours a day.

As I became better acquainted with the Phoenix area, I thought the Shadow Mountains would be just the place for the prayer chapel of my dreams, so I began to look into making the dream a reality. As years passed, my congregation began to share my dream with me. Donations came in, some of them quite unexpectedly. One woman, much like the New Testament widow whom Jesus credited with giving her last "widow's mite," sent us a small donation with a note, "Poor as this offering may be, it is my very best-ever gift to the Lord. This is for Mount Prayer!"

But something happened to change the course of my dream. The city wrote a letter, advising us that the area on which we planned to construct the chapel had been declared a "mountain preserve." The eleven acres belonged to us, but we would not be permitted to build on them.

After praying and discussing the matter with our lawyers, I was invited to address the city council. I told them in detail what our plans involved. I made it clear that through the chapel's crisis telephone lines and follow-up ministry, the hungry would be fed, the poor would be clothed, and the desperate would receive emotional and spiritual assistance.

All this happened around the time that several highly visible Christian leaders fell into disgrace. Their stories made front-page news from coast to coast. As far as the media was concerned, it was open season on ministries—and ours was no exception. The local papers reported (I should say *mis*-reported) that I wanted to build a seventy-foot prayer tower, á la Oral Roberts, on Shadow Mountain!

I responded with calls and explanations, describing exactly what our humble chapel with its simple cross would look like. But by then the political cartoonists had started in. Day after day, the prayer chapel was mocked in caricatures that depicted me as an egotistical promoter and greedy fund-raiser. The mayor stood up for me and confronted the media with charges of irresponsibility. But the chapel never got built.

Will our little prayer chapel ever exist? Yes, it will. I believe that dream came from God and that God will bring it to pass. I don't know when, and I don't know where, but someday Phoenix will have a prayer chapel—and it will be proof to all believers that a dream delayed is not a dream denied.

God's Dream of Restoration

ONE OF THE MOST DIFFICULT PERIODS I'VE ENCOUNTERED IN my ministry came in the days and weeks after the very public fall of two men of God—Jim Bakker and Jimmy Swaggart. Those were heartbreaking months for me. Bakker and Swaggart were my friends—and a friend, I believe, is a gift from God—and is forever. I agonized and prayed for hours and hours that God would take care of them, show them how they had failed, and draw them to Himself.

Meanwhile, apart from the personal sorrow involved, I had to contend with the intense media interest in my denomination, the Assemblies of God, to which both Bakker and Swaggart belonged. Since Phoenix First Assembly is one of the largest Assemblies of God churches in the country, we were soon inundated with journalists, talk show hosts, anchormen and women, and even tabloid reporters. The phone messages piled up on my desk: *Crossfire... Nightline...* CNN. They all wanted to talk to me, to get my "perspective," my "reaction," and my "personal feelings."

I wasn't sure what to do, so I prayed for wisdom. Clearly I felt the Lord say, "Don't talk. You don't need to be in touch with them. Instead, go up on that mountain behind the church and hide yourself with Me."

I obeyed—and I'm so glad I did. That became one of the most spiritually productive times of my life. I experienced the greatest growth in grace I'd ever known. The world was saying, "That's the end of that kind of fundamentalism."

God was saying, "I'm the God of new beginnings!"

When I went to the mountain and prayed, God gave me a miraculous sense of peace. He taught me to trust Him, to forgive, and, most importantly, to restore. I learned on the side of that mountain that the battle is not over until the person who fell is restored to a full relationship with the Lord Jesus Christ. That is what was on the heart of God during those dark days—God wanted to see His fallen sons back in close communion with Him.

In the years that followed, God brought this dream to pass. Today Jim Bakker is living at the Dream Center in Los Angeles—in one of the former nun's quarters. His son lives in a room next to his. On Jim's other side lives a convicted murderer, and next to him lives a former drug addict. Jim Bakker is doing for others what God did for him: restoring broken men and women to Jesus. That's what the Dream Center is all about—the restoration of broken lives and broken dreams. That's what God wants most of all. That's why He sent His Son.

A Dream Reunion

ONE MORNING WHILE I WAS HAVING MY DEVOTIONS, GOD told me to do something I wasn't sure I wanted to do. My reading that day was from Matthew 25:35–36, where Jesus says, "For I was hungry and you gave me something to eat, I was thirsty and you gave me something to drink...I was in prison and you came to visit me" (NIV). As I read I knew God wanted me to go visit Jim Bakker in prison. Now I had known Jim for years and counted him among my friends, but I wasn't sure visiting him was such a good idea. But the Lord was persistent: "Go visit Jim Bakker."

Obedient but somewhat uneasy, I got on a plane, flew to Minneapolis, and drove out into the country where the prison was located. Jim greeted me with tears in his eyes. "Thank you so much for coming," he said. "I don't have many visitors. First Billy Graham came, and now you've come, too." At that point I figured I was in pretty good company.

Jim and I visited for three hours, and when it was time

for me to go, he asked me if I'd do him a favor. Jim explained that when he went to prison and his marriage broke up, his teenage son, Jamie, began a downward spiral into drugs and alcohol. "Could you get him to Phoenix and into the Master's Commission at your church (a dicipleship program for youth)?" he asked me. Of course, I agreed to help. But later when I called Jamie, the angry young man made it clear that he wasn't at all interested.

Several years passed, and Jim Bakker got out of prison. He moved into a secluded cottage in North Carolina, which, along with a car, had been provided for him by Franklin Graham, Billy Graham's son and the director of a wonderful ministry called Samaritan's Purse. Jim called me and asked for my help again. "Jamie's living with me now," he explained, "but he's using drugs and alcohol, and we're kind of crossways with each other. Can you bring him to Phoenix?"

"I called him when you asked me to before," I explained, "but he doesn't want to come to Phoenix."

"Yes, he does. Now he wants to come."

We flew Jamie out to Phoenix and put him in the home of Mike Wall and his wife, who head up a ministry for "skater kids." The second week there Jamie came forward at the invitation to rededicate his life to Jesus. Soon he was involved with Mike in his ministry to skaters, punkers, and other "alternative kids" with strange hair, clothes, tattoos, and pierced body parts.

Every year at our pastors' conference, which hosts more than seven thousand pastors and workers from all around the world, we feature some of the ministries in our church. That year we decided to feature Mike Wall's ministry to teenagers, and Jamie wanted to give his testimony.

"I haven't told anybody who you are," I reminded him. "I've been trying to protect you from the media and the crowd. Are you sure you want them to know?"

"It's okay," Jamie told me. "I want to come out and tell my story."

Meanwhile, Jim Bakker had just about decided to stay out of the public eye for the rest of his life. He didn't have the confidence he needed to face people, and he was very frightened by the media. "Prison," he explained to me, "is such a destructive place. Every day the system tells you that you're no good." Jim was demoralized and could not imagine that he would ever again have a dream from God.

I wrote him and told him about the upcoming conference and Jamie's planned testimony. I suggested that he come and hear his son speak. We talked on the phone a few days later. "I think it would hurt you if I came," he told me. "The media would jump all over you."

Jim obviously longed to see his son, but he didn't want to hurt our church and me by his presence. "Jim," I told him firmly, "I don't care what you did. A man has a right to hear his son give his testimony. I want you to be here."

Then Jim said, "But suppose I came and sat in another building? Or, what if I sat in the back where no one could see me?"

I finally convinced Jim that he would be welcome. "Don't tell Jamie," Jim said as we finished our conversation. I didn't tell Jamie or anybody else about our plans. No one knew but Jim Bakker and Tommy Barnett.

The night of his testimony, when Jamie came up to the mike and explained who he was, the people applauded with a great standing ovation. I hadn't known what to expect, but I was pleased to see that they were warmly receptive. After he finished, I got up and said, "You know, Jamie, your dad called, and he wanted to be here tonight." I went through our conversation, all the uncertainties we'd discussed, and then finally announced, "Jamie, your dad is here with us."

Jim Bakker stood up and hesitantly walked to the front of the sanctuary where he took his son in his arms and held him close, both of them weeping openly. As one, over seven thousand pastors jumped to their feet, applauded, and wept. They cried out, "Jim, we love you!" For several minutes the applause continued nonstop as the prodigal son and the prodigal father were reunited.

That night was a dream come true for all of us. God had fulfilled His plan for reconciliation, His plan for forgiveness, for a fallen man and his wounded son.

A Son's Dream Come True

WHEN JIM BAKKER SPOKE AT THE PASTORS' CONFERENCE, HE told about his relationship with his son Jamie, who was standing next to him, gripping his father's arm. "I went to prison," Jim told the stunned audience, "and Jamie couldn't come to visit me by himself until his sixteenth birthday. The first day he was old enough to come, he arrived in the morning and stayed all day. What a great day we had! When it came time for lock-down, Jamie had to leave.

"'Dad,' he told me as he embraced me and said goodbye, 'this has been the greatest day of my whole life. All I ever wanted is to have you all to myself for one whole day. Today was like a dream come true for me!'"

Jim Bakker could hardly speak, so deep were his feelings. And he went on to say some of the most sobering words those pastors would ever hear: "I had to go to prison for my boy to spend one day with me," he told them. "Pastors! Don't gain the whole world and lose your sons!"

For a few moments, Jim wept with Jamie. Then he continued, "I've met many famous people in my lifetime. I've stood on the same platform with the president of the United States and met with senators. I was building the largest Christian ministry in the United States.

"But while I was in prison somebody sent me a picture. There I was, standing in front of all my great buildings at PTL in a hard hat—ready to launch into another building program. And there, behind me, was the shadow of a little boy with his arms wrapped around my leg. He was holding on to his dad. Men," he repeated, *"do not win the world and lose your own sons and daughters!"*

After that unforgettable message from Jim Bakker, I asked all the pastors whose dreams had failed to come forward and pray with Jim and Jamie. Literally hundreds of pastors streamed down the aisles. Some of them stayed in the church all night, praying and pleading with God to restore their own families, their ministries, and their dreams. Jim Bakker had hardly dared to hope that his own failings could help others avoid failure. But by God's grace, that's exactly what happened.

Jim Bakker and the Dream Center

AFTER HIS REUNION WITH HIS SON IN PHOENIX, JIM BAKKER agreed to speak to the people at the Dream Center. I wanted him to see what we were doing in Los Angeles and share his testimony. He came on a Thursday night, and he told me afterward that he had never felt such love in all his life. "Absolute, total love," he said in amazement. "After spending my last few years in prison, to experience a true New Testament body of Christ is just awesome."

When he spoke to the men and women in L.A, Jim was simply preaching to hurting people. They didn't care that he'd fallen; in fact, he could better relate to them because he had. More than half the people raised their hands when he asked, "How many of you have been in prison?" He told them with a big smile, "I've never felt more at home than I feel here."

And Jim Bakker had never before preached the way he preached that night. He was powerfully anointed, and the response to his message was overwhelming. After that first night he asked me, "Could I stay at the Dream Center another day?"

"Of course," I told him. "We'll put you in a hotel."

"Oh, no, I don't want to go to a hotel. I want to stay right here."

We gave him a room, and that night he went out with a team that picks up runaway kids in Hollywood. We've learned that if runaways are not reached within the first two weeks after they leave home, they get caught in the deadly web of drugs, prostitution, and pimps. So Jim Bakker went out on the streets, and, along with the others, he brought kids back. He ministered to them for three hours. Every time he tried to stop, the kids begged him not to go. At the closing, Jim shared that he had been sexually abused as a young boy. Every kid there said, "Yeah, me, too."

When every young man began to call out "me, too!" Jim realized why the Holy Spirit had prompted him to share his own most painful secret that night. Even the youth counselors began to share their own stories of abuse. God had granted Jim Bakker "instantaneous identification," enabling him to reach those kids with God's unconditional love and grace.

Jim asked me again, "Would you mind if I stayed one more day?" The next afternoon he went out with the bus to Skid Row. The men there didn't care if he'd made a mistake or two. They'd made a few of their own.

"Can I stay another night?" he asked. He stayed, and the next day he went out with a feeding program and preached in the street. People accepted Christ. He asked to stay another day.

"Don't make the kind of mistakes I've made," he told the Dream Center audience. "God caused me to lose everything, and it sent me into a tailspin." People of all ages came forward and gave their lives to Christ when he was done.

At the end of his eighth night in Los Angeles, Jim said, "Tommy, I want to ask you a question. I don't want to hurt you. But would you consider letting me come and live at the Dream Center? I have had many lucrative offers from scores of ministries and contract offers to be on television. But I don't want another TV program—I don't want to go back to that! I choose to be right here. The only time in my ministry that I've felt loved and happy is here. I just want to heal hurting people like I did the last few days. Will you let me have a few rooms to fix up? I want to help restore fallen preachers. If I could take them out to the streets and let them minister to others the way I've done these past few days, I *know* it would heal them as well as myself. This is the only place I feel truly loved. Will you let me stay?"

Of course Matthew and I were delighted to have Jim Bakker stay with us at the Dream Center. We gave him a room to live in and some rooms for his new ministry—helping other ministers who have failed. All he wants to do is to help others.

Today, like so many others in Los Angeles—including his son, Jamie—Jim Bakker is dreaming again. And in response, God is restoring his life and using his past to lead others into a better future.

With a Dream You Can Make It!

ONE NIGHT A YOUNG MAN ATTENDED THE YOUTH MEETING at the Dream Center and responded to the invitation to come forward to accept Jesus as his personal Savior. That night Manuel gave his heart to Jesus and was saved.

As Manuel prayed with the youth workers at the altar, the discouraging details of his life began to emerge. His dad was a drug user who had contracted AIDS. Manuel's mother, unable to deal with the abuse of drugs any longer, had left, leaving Manuel, a fifteen-year-old boy, alone with his father. Manuel was ashamed of his father, and their relationship had broken down—each closing himself off in his own private despair.

But after Manuel accepted Jesus as his Savior, he was determined to be restored in his relationship with his father. He brought his father to church, where his father also accepted Jesus as his Savior. But the disease of AIDS continued to ravage his father's body.

"How can there be a God, if He would destroy my dad?" Manuel cried out to the youth pastor. "He's all I've got. If he dies, I'll be without parents—without anybody in the whole world!"

The youth pastor prayed diligently with Manuel for several hours—to no avail. Manuel could not find peace. Finally, about 10 P.M. the youth pastor sent someone to knock gently on Jim Bakker's door. "Can you help?" the worker asked. "We have been praying with Manuel, but nothing seems to help him."

Jim immediately dressed and went to talk with Manuel. For the next hour and a half he tried to give Manuel every promise he could find in God's Word. But none of it seemed to bring any hope to Manuel.

In desperation Jim felt led to share his own story with Manuel. "At one time I had three thousand people working for me," Jim said. "I had beautiful homes, cars, even a seventy-foot boat. But overnight I lost everything."

Then, as Jim's voice began to break, he continued. "From the middle of prison I watched on television as my home burned to the ground. Then I found out that my wife—the one I loved the most—was divorcing me to marry the man I had thought was my best friend." He looked right into Manuel's eyes and repeated, "Manuel, I lost the one I loved the most. But today I love Jesus more than ever. He *never* left me, *never* forsook me. Jesus promised in His Word that He would *never, never* leave me or forsake me—and He hasn't."

Manuel listened carefully to Jim's story. He looked right at Jim and said, "Mr. Bakker, if you could make it, then I know I will be able to make it, too!"

At that moment one of the greatest healings in Jim Bakker's life took place. All the pain of his prison years faded away as he looked in that boy's face. He realized that God was turning the pain of his own experience into positive gain—God was using *him* to help others!

A few days later Manuel's father died, and Matthew preached his funeral. The people at the Dream Center took up a collection and bought Manuel one of the required school uniforms so he could attend school at the Dream Center.

Manuel's newfound faith in God saw him through. He thanked God for his salvation and for his father's salvation. He moved into the Dream Center where he lives today. Everyone at the center—staff and people in the various programs—"adopted" Manuel as one of their own. Because Jim Bakker learned to dream again—Manuel did, too!

Bringing Dreams to Life

ONE OF MY FAVORITE EXPRESSIONS IS A SIMPLE, TWO-WORD statement: *Finish Strong!* To me this means that we shouldn't give up before we bring forth the fruit of our dreams—with God's help, of course.

One of my favorite illustrations of this idea is the story of three evangelists who were ministry dynamos in the mid-1940s.

The first man's name was Chuck Templeton. One seminary president described him as the most gifted, talented young preacher in America. One magazine enthused that he was the "Babe Ruth of evangelism."

The second man's name was Bron Clifford. He too was a powerhouse in the pulpit. People lined up to hear him. In fact, at Baylor University, the bells in the clocktower were disabled so his sermon would not be disrupted. By the time he reached his mid-twenties, Clifford had broken more attendance records, ministered to more national leaders, and led more souls to Christ than anyone in our country's history. He even caught Hollywood's attention—they wanted to make him a film star.

The third man's name was Billy Graham. As most people know by now, he was propelled into fame from the moment he first set foot on the revival circuit. His crusades became legendary almost immediately. And they still are.

But what about the other two?

Templeton left the ministry at the dawn of the 1950s. He turned to radio announcing and broadcast journalism. And not long after he left the pulpit, he left the Lord who had placed him there. He declared himself an atheist and vanished from public view.

Bron Clifford's life ended tragically after he lost his battle with alcoholism. Clifford also lost his family—including two Down's syndrome children—because of his financial irresponsibility. He died in a run-down motel of cirrhosis of the liver, alone, broke, and forgotten. He was only thirty-five years old.

I've told these stories again and again. And along with them, I have quoted a shocking statistic: Only one out of ten who start in ministry at the age of twenty-one serve the Lord to age sixty-five. Why do they fall away? They fall into sin or succumb to emotional pain, bad theology, financial greed, or other worldly attractions.

But people in public ministry and full-time Christian service aren't the only ones who are susceptible to seeing their dreams of godliness disintegrate. All Christians face the same temptations encountered by pastors, ministers, and priests. In fact, every Christian has to choose—daily, hourly, moment by moment—whom we will serve. Only in faithfulness to God, reliance on the Spirit, and conformity to the example of Jesus can we bring our dreams to life. Only through Him can we finish strong. In the Christian life, it's not how you start—it's how you finish.

Your Walk With God Can Be Even Deeper...

With *Charisma* magazine, you'll be informed and inspired by the features and stories about what the Holy Spirit is doing in the lives of believers today.

Each issue:

- Brings you exclusive world-wide reports to rejoice over.
- Keeps you informed on the latest news from a Christian perspective.
- Includes miracle-filled testimonies to build your faith.
- Gives you access to relevant teaching and exhortation from the most respected Christian leaders of our day.